ALSO BY KIESE LAYMON

Heavy: An American Memoir

Long Division: A Novel

HOW TO SLOWLY KILL YOURSELF AND OTHERS IN AMERICA

ESSAYS

KIESE LAYMON

SCRIBNER

New York   London   Toronto   Sydney   New Delhi

Scribner
An Imprint of Simon & Schuster, Inc.
1230 Avenue of the Americas
New York, NY 10020

This Scribner trade paperback edition November 2020

SCRIBNER and design are registered trademarks of The Gale Group, Inc., used under license by Simon & Schuster, Inc., the publisher of this work.

For information about special discounts for bulk purchases, please contact Simon & Schuster Special Sales at 1-866-506-1949 or business@simonandschuster.com.

The Simon & Schuster Speakers Bureau can bring authors to your live event. For more information or to book an event, contact the Simon & Schuster Speakers Bureau at 1-866-248-3049 or visit our website at www.simonspeakers.com.

Manufactured in the United States of America

1   3   5   7   9   10   8   6   4   2

Library of Congress Cataloging-in-Publication Data has been applied for.

ISBN 978-1-9821-7082-0
ISBN 978-1-9821-7083-7 (ebook)

Special thanks to the following publications for including these essays in their pages (in this or an earlier form): "Mississippi: An Awakening, in Days," published in *Vanity Fair*; "What I Pledge Allegiance To," published in *The Fader*; "Da Art of Storytellin' (A Prequel)," published in *Oxford American*; "How They Do in Oxford" and "Daydreaming with D'Andre Brown," published in ESPN.com; "Hey Mama" and "You Are the Second Person," published in *Guernica*; "Hip-Hop Stole My Southern Black Boy," published in *Hip Hop Reader*; "Our Kind of Ridiculous," "How to Slowly Kill Yourself and Others in America," "The Worst of White Folks," and "We Will Never Ever Know," published in *Gawker*.

Certain names and identifying details have been changed.

For Uncle Jimmy, both of them

"You don't tell all the secrets when you're trying to get free."

—Imani Perry

CONTENTS

Author's Note #2   xi

Mississippi: An Awakening, in Days   1

What I Pledge Allegiance To   21

Da Art of Storytellin' (A Prequel)   31

How They Do in Oxford   41

Hey Mama: An Essay in Emails   55

Echo: Mychal, Darnell, Kiese, Kai, and Marlon   67

Daydreaming with D'Andre Brown   79

You Are the Second Person   89

Hip-Hop Stole My Southern Black Boy   103

Our Kind of Ridiculous   115

How to Slowly Kill Yourself and Others in America   125

The Worst of White Folks   139

We Will Never Ever Know   149

AUTHOR'S NOTE #2

Yesterday, I attended a virtual book club where *Heavy: An American Memoir* was being read. When I clicked the link to join the Zoom, I saw the faces, necks, and shoulders of seven beautiful pixelated Black women from as far west as Las Vegas and as far east as Long Island. I assumed from their familiarity they'd all gone to school together. They told me they just met at the beginning of the pandemic. The seven women were initially part of a two-thousand-person book club that shrank to one hundred people for reasons no one would explain. Eventually, the seven women decided to create their own virtual book club.

Ten minutes into the conversation, after everyone had checked in, the organizer of the Zoom said they'd all recently met in person, gathering in Chicago a few weeks ago.

I was confused.

"A few weeks ago," I said into my greasy computer screen, "we were still deep in COVID."

"We quarantined for two weeks at home," one of the women said. "Then we all went to Chicago and stayed with the organizer in the middle of the pandemic."

"Wait, wait, wait," I said. "Y'all risked it all for a book club?"

The seven women looked at each other and filled that space with full-bodied laughter, wet eyes, and smiles that rocked back, back, forth, and forth.

They risked it all for the radical possibilities of friendships forged in books.

I understood.

I was twenty-eight years old, without a literary agent, when I was offered my first publishing deal. Though I'd never met the editor interested in my work, I assumed all editors wanted to be friends with the writers whose work they respected. I knew I desperately wanted to be friends with any editor who respected me. I realized, nearly a decade too late, that this editor was never my friend.

Shamefully, I would repeat this pattern of assumed friendship in publishing with folks who, to their credit, never called me a friend. The only thing I did remotely well during my failed relationships with publishing was read, write, and reread. Rereading *The Bluest Eye* taught me how to value what I'd been told I could not see. Rereading *The Fire Next Time* taught me how to value the messy work of love in America. Rereading *Going to the Territory* taught me that "human being" was a verb. Rereading *Kindred* taught me to will my husky Black body beyond spectacle and into a generative space that needed to look back, back, forth, and forth.

Not only had every friendship in my adult life been forged by books, I literally found radical friendship in the authors and texts I imaginatively met. Pecola Breedlove, Nicholas Scoby, and Esch were my best friends. The first and last lines in "The Cask of Amontillado" were my shady white friends. Toni Cade Bambara and Richard Wright were my super oldhead friends. I walked with my friends, talked with friends. We spent tens of thousands of hours in each other's homes, wandering around each other's guts.

I started this book the week after my uncle Jimmy died in July 2007. It was initially called *On Parole*. I wrote half of the essays for the book lying on my back from a faculty apartment in Poughkeepsie, New York. The essays were posted on a blog called *Cold Drank*. I started writing to my uncle Jimmy because I thought his was the only ghost who might understand the contours of the fiery tent of shame I'd made for myself. I wanted "We Will Never Ever Know," the essay directly addressed to my uncle, to end the book. I wanted the book to read backward, from now to its origins.

We had one problem. I was terrified of *now*. Now looked ugly, like me.

While my relationship with paragraphs, chapters, and dead authors was getting more intimate, I was getting worse at being human. One cold night in New York, in 2009, a friend I loved told me that I was precisely the kind of human being I claimed to despise, the kind of friend who fed off mangling the possibilities of radical friendship. I defended myself against this truth and really against responsibility, as American monsters, American murderers, American cheaters, and American friends tend to do, and I tried to make this person feel as absolutely malignant as I was. Later that night, I could not sleep, and for the first time in my life, I wrote the sentence, "I've been slowly killing myself and others close to me."

The first draft of *How to Slowly Kill Yourself and Others in America* ended with an essay called "You Are the Second Person." It was the only essay in the book unafraid of assessing from whence the actual writing on the page came. I never wanted "You Are the Second Person" to end the book, but I hadn't willed myself to write rigorously about where and why I was in the world after my publishing failures.

I wanted the book to be a site of the catastrophic and pleasurable, the intellectual and the everyday, the public and the private, the awkwardly destructive and the wholly sublime. Instead of imagining standard "literary" audiences, I knew that I wanted to question traditional literary forms and trajectories by writing to friends, and sensibilities, who didn't like to read, and friends, and sensibilities, who were paid to read for a living. I knew that I wanted to create work that explored, with colorful profundity and comedy, the reckless order of American *human* being, especially since so much of the nation was in a dizzying rush to crown itself multicultural, post-racial, and mostly innocent. I wanted to create a book with a self-reflexive musty Mississippi blues ethos. I wanted a book that could be read, and really heard, front to back, back to front, in one sitting. I wanted readers to generate art in response to this text while working with the essays at being better lovers of those we profess to love. The hardest part, of course, is that I wanted to become a person, not just an author, worthy of forgiveness and risk from literary and literal friends.

Though I was forty-two years old when I approached the publisher about buying this book back, revising and reissuing it the way I always imagined, far too old to believe in the sanctity of professional friendships, I still believed that the people with whom you collaborated on art were friends. I still believed that the white folks we made money for owed us friendship, or at least relationships with a pinch of integrity. I was still begging white folks in publishing to be better to me than I was to friends I claimed to love.

Today, in the midst of the most death-filled summer of our lives, I bought my first two books back from the publisher so I could revise and reissue them. I paid ten times what the publisher initially paid for the books. I'm thinking a lot about debt, reparation, vengeance, residue, and the tendrils of humiliation caused and withstood. I am thankful to have made it to a place where I will never waste my words on anyone in publishing whom I burdened with the hope of friendship. As painful as the publishing experience has been, I have radically loving friendships with the folks whom I currently collaborate with on art.

Revision did that.

In this revision, I start in Mississippi, where I am actually writing in 2020, and I hope that the reader works their way back to the beginning which, for me, is always the end. The middle though—all those middles of all those essays and all those real and imagined friendships—is where we find the guts. I hope you find radical possibilities and guts galore in this revised piece of art. Writing the first edition of *How to Slowly Kill Yourself and Others in America* brought me back to Mississippi, literally and literarily. Coming home to Mississippi had given me the space to finish *Heavy*. In the revision of this book, I write from Mississippi about our current awakening. The movement of the essays is painted in regret and revelry. All the pieces in this book are differently shaped, paced, and greased with orange-red odes to my Grandmama and her generation of Black women in Mississippi. The book moves backward, in a counterclockwise migration, from North Mississippi, to Upstate New York, to Pennsylvania, to Ohio, to Central Mississippi. It marches from the wandering weirdness of middle age, to lonely collaborations born of saccharine dreams, to the toxicity of American responsibility heaped on Black children and elders. These essays want us to have radical friendships rooted in courage and healthy choices. When I've had courage, I often lacked the healthy choices. When I've had healthy choices, I often lacked courage. Ending unhealthy transactional relationships and opening ourselves to radical possibilities is one way we effectively heal ourselves and others in America. Securing the rights to my books, revising them, and publishing them the way they want to be published are the most loving acts I could do for my work, my body, and my Mississippi.

I hope no writer alive ever has to pay ten times what they were paid to secure the rights to a piece of art that helped them, and others, accept life. If nothing else, I hope every writer alive never ceases believing in the rugged majesty of revision.

I wanted it all to stop. I needed it all to stop. I revised. I revised. I stopped it.

MISSISSIPPI:
AN AWAKENING, IN DAYS

DAY 1

22 Americans are dead from coronavirus, and Donald Trump tweets, "We have a perfectly coordinated and fine tuned plan at the White House for our attack on CoronaVirus."

I hear from Joe Osmundson, writer, friend, and scientist, that I should not attend the Association of Writers Programs, a conference I say I am too tired to attend, a conference where I will not be paid for attending. "The government is way behind on this," Joe writes. "Experts in our community are the best we have. I've been talking to a lot of friends working on this, and I trust them a lot."

"Should I fly, fam?" I ask him.

"It's not 'US' we're doing this for," he texts back. "The risk for you is still low, but it's kinda like what do we owe our elders and the folks with compromised immune systems."

"Thanks for this," I write back. "I'ma sit my ass at home and not go to these other events on my schedule."

These other events are paid readings I'm supposed to do in Ohio and West Virginia. These events are where I make most of my money. The first event in Ohio is sold out, but I tell myself that I'm sure they'll postpone before the tenth. I assume the same thing about West Virginia.

I am lonely. I am afraid.

And/Yet/But/Somehow I drive to the casino in Tunica, Mississippi, one of the poorest counties in the United States, and lather my hands in sanitizer.

It could all be so much worse.

DAY 2

31 Americans are dead from coronavirus, and after meeting with Republican leaders, Donald Trumps says, "It's about twenty-six deaths, within our country. And had we not acted quickly, that number would have been substantially more."

These paid events I am booked to attend have yet to be canceled. It took Grandmama, the person who will get most of the money I make for these trips, a year working in the chicken plant to make the kind of money that awaits me for these two events.

Grandmama is one of the elders Joe talked about. She is a ninety-year-old Black woman from Mississippi, and her immune system is severely compromised. She believes she is still alive because of hard work and Jesus Christ.

I have my agency tell the folks in Cincinnati that I will not under any circumstance be signing books or shaking hands at the event.

We all have to be safe.

Later that night, I sign books. I shake hands. I hug people. I feel love. I lather my hands in sanitizer. A monied man at the event gives me a ticket to see Lauryn Hill, who is also in Cincinnati. I tell organizers of the event that I'd rather go to the Lauryn Hill show than go to dinner.

I skip Lauryn Hill.

I skip dinner.

I congratulate myself on skipping both, on looking out for

elders, and people like my Grandmama with compromised immune systems.

It could all be so much worse.

DAY 3

38 Americans are dead from coronavirus, and Donald Trump says, in his address to the nation, "The virus will not have a chance against us. No nation is more prepared or more resilient than the United States."

I am outside of my hotel in Cincinnati, waiting for a car service to drive me to Marshall, West Virginia. When the lanky old white man with large knuckles pulls up, I place my bags in his trunk. I do not shake his hand. Neither he nor I have on a mask or gloves. I am headed to West Virginia to get this money in the backseat of a new black car driven by an old white man.

I lather my hands in sanitizer.

Barely out of Cincinnati, the driver tells me he is a preacher. We talk about his church, his calling, his time living in the Bronx, his wife's abusive upbringing, all the powerful men he's driven place to place. He stops talking for a bit, and I look at the land we're zooming by. I am a writer. I should be writing about land I've never seen. I lather my hands in sanitizer, open my phone to type a sentence.

"It could all be so much worse," I write.

I get to West Virginia two hours before I'm supposed to have dinner with the organizers of tonight's event. Kristen walks me from the hotel around the corner to the restaurant. There is a long table of around ten folks already sitting down.

"How y'all doing?" I ask, faking a laugh. "I guess we're not doing handshakes, huh?"

I am forever a fat Black boy from Jackson, Mississippi. I

hate to be trapped in white places where I do not know anyone Black. My mama and Grandmama rarely sit with their backs to doors. I choose the seat at the end of the table, next to a young brother whose hairline makes me remember Mississippi.

Under the table, I lather my hands in sanitizer.

I am sitting across from two powerful white people whose rhythms I cannot pick up. I cannot tell when they will laugh, when they will fidget. I cannot tell if they have actually laughed or fidgeted. The white woman in front of me does not want to be there. I find out that the university is preparing to suspend in-person classes and begin distance learning.

No one is coming to this reading tonight, I tell myself. That's definitely for the better, as long as I can still get my check.

I order a Thai cauliflower wrap and fries. There is no way I'm eating that wrap. Or the fries.

I have eaten all but one of the fries when the brilliant brother with the familiar hairline offers me some sanitizer.

"You think we could shake hands now?" he asks.

"Oh absolutely," I say, and shake the hands of all the incredible students, thanking everyone for wanting to come out in such a scary time.

I ask for a to-go box for my wrap and say that I hope to see y'all at the reading. On the way to the reading, I stop back by the hotel because I don't need my backpack smelling like old cauliflower. White people treat Black people who smell like old cauliflower like Black people.

I'm scared. I'm tired. I'm lonely. I need my check. I don't want to be treated like a Black person by white people while trying to dodge coronavirus.

It's hot in my room. I'm sweating way too much. I take off the shirt beneath my Meager hoodie. It's drenched. I place the cauliflower wrap on the counter.

I think I have coronavirus.

Or I'm just fat. Or I'm just nervous.

I think I have coronavirus.

I get to the venue. The white woman who greets me walks with a limp. I walk with a limp. She kindly takes me to the green room. A gentle tall white man knocks on the green room door and pulls out a huge bottle of sanitizer.

"Your agency told us you needed this."

"Oh wow," I say, trying to act like I had no idea. "That's weird. Thanks."

After the reading, some of the astounding students whom I had dinner with come on stage and ask me to sign their books, take pictures, shake hands. I sign their books, take pictures, shake hands. I walk out to the foyer, sit at a table, and sign more books. After all the books are signed, I walk out and meet the gentle tall white man who gave me the sanitizer. He is going to be taking me back to my hotel in his truck.

We talk about coronavirus. We talk about Randy Moss. We talk about Jason Williams. We talk about coronavirus.

As we get to my hotel, I'm wondering whether I'm supposed to shake his hand since I'm convinced both of us have coronavirus.

The tall gentle white man keeps both hands on the steering wheel and tells me bye.

"Thanks," I say out loud.

My room smells like old cauliflower. I take two showers, lather my hands in sanitizer, and I try to dream.

DAY 4

40 Americans are dead from coronavirus, and Mississippi governor Tate Reeves is cutting short his European vacation because of Donald Trump's European travel restrictions.

At five in the morning, another white man picks me up to drive me to the airport. He does not speak. I give him a big tip when he drops me off. He holds the money like I'd hold a boogery Kleenex given to me by a white man driving me to an airport.

"Thanks," I say out loud.

I am wearing a black hoodie, a black hat, a black Bane mask, black headphones. Hanging around my neck are two dog tags. One, a quote from James Baldwin, says, "The very time I thought I was lost my dungeon shook and my chains fell off." The other, a quote from Lucille Clifton, says, "they ask me to remember but they want me to remember their memories and i keep on remembering mine."

I take a selfie on the plane and place it on Instagram with the caption: "Strange times when you have to be on the road to make money to help care for a miraculous 90 year old woman who you won't be able to touch for 14 days . . . Kindness. Tenderness. Generosity. We can do this."

Fourteen days, I tell myself. It could all be so much worse.

"The virus will not have a chance against us," Donald Trump says later that afternoon.

DAY 5

413 Americans are dead from coronavirus, and Donald Trump will not say, "I am sorry."

Governor Tate Reeves decides that the one abortion clinic in Mississippi is not an essential business that should remain open, but gun stores are. I've written around Tate without saying Tate's name for eight years.

In college, my partner, Nzola, and I got into an altercation with two fraternities on Bid Day. Some fraternity members wore Confederate capes, Afro wigs, and others blackened their faces. I've written about how they called us "niggers." I've written about how they called Nzola a "nigger b—." I've written about that experience and guns. I've written about that experience and bats. I've written about that experience and how my investment in patriarchy diminished Nzola's suffering.

I have never written about the heartbreak of seeing the future governor of Mississippi in that group of white boys, proudly representing the Kappa Alpha fraternity and its Confederate commitment to Black suffering. I have never admitted that after playing basketball against Tate all through high school, and knowing that he went to a public school called Florence, not a segregation academy, like so many other white boys we knew, it hurt my feelings to see Tate doing what white boys who pledged their identities to the Old South ideologies were supposed to do.

When I saw Tate in that Confederate cacophony of drunken white boyhood, doing what they did, I knew he could one day be governor of Mississippi and President of the United States.

That is still the most damning thing I can ever say about a white boy from Mississippi.

DAY 6

9,400 Americans are dead from coronavirus, and Donald Trump will not say, "I was wrong."

Mama is scared because the nurse we pay to take care of Grandmama will not wear her mask for fear that it could hurt my Grandmama's feelings.

I am scared because Mama will not stop going to work. She sends me a eulogy she wants me to read if she dies. The eulogy confuses me. There is so much left out. She wants people to know her dream was to be of use to the world, and particularly Mississippi. But the eulogy is more about the places Mama has been than the justice work she's done. I do not argue with Mama. I tell her that if she dies before I die, I will read the eulogy as it is written.

It could all be so much worse.

I get an email from the writer Cherry Lou Sy, saying that one of those dead 9,400 Americans is my former student Kimarlee Nguyen. Kimarlee and I shared a classroom at Vassar College. Long before she was my student, Kimarlee would greet me with this raspy offering:

"Yo, Kiese!"

When we finally shared a classroom, I was unable to adequately protect Kimarlee from the phantoms haunting most American classrooms. Phantoms need hosts. Many white hosts need phantoms. These phantoms encouraged Kimarlee to write her Cambodian self out of her writing. They disciplined her for not erasing her family's rememories of Khmer Rouge.

Kimarlee accepted her sadness, her fatigue, her anger, and then along with James and Charmaine, she willed herself to write more deeply into the historic imagination of ancestral spirits.

I always assumed coronavirus would take my Grandmama, my mama, my aunties, my friends, me, possibly in reverse order.

I never ever assumed it would take my students.

DAY 7

104,051 Americans are dead from the coronavirus, and Donald Trump will not say, "I am sorry." After Darnella Frazier, a seventeen-year-old Black girl from South Minneapolis, courageously films police executing a survivor of coronavirus named

George Floyd, and Breonna Taylor, an EMT tasked with aiding those with coronavirus, is shot by police five times in her own house, uprisings begin in the United States.

The week before savvy, young, mostly Black folks longing to breathe and break fill Jackson, Mississippi, streets, a lone white Jewish teacher in Oxford, Mississippi, cuts his hands and places bloody handprints all over the biggest Confederate monument on the campus of "Ole Miss." The Jewish brother spray-paints "spiritual genocide" on all four sides of the monument before being arrested.

Instead of covering the monument, workers are told to cover "spiritual genocide" with what looks like swaddling cloth.

I help bail the Jewish brother out. I help bail out folks in Mississippi, in Minneapolis, in Louisville.

I go home alone.

I am forty-five years old, the exact age Grandmama was when I was born. Just like Grandmama at forty-five, I live alone in Mississippi. Yet unlike Grandmama, I have no children, no grandchildren. I own no land, no garden, no property, and I am afraid of walking in my neighborhood under the light of a moon or sun.

This should not haunt me. But phantoms move at their own speed.

I sit in this house, once the site of a Confederate mansion, alone, afraid to go outside, afraid to let anyone outside see me.

I am more successful than I've ever imagined. Yet, I am terrified of sleeping because my body no longer knows how to dream. I know that people die in their dreams. I am not afraid of death. I am afraid of being killed while dreaming. Driving while Black. Jogging while Black. Dreaming while Black. Fighting while Black. Loving while Black. I wonder if movement, mobility, love are the features of Black life the worst of white Americans most despise.

DAY 8

108,278 Americans are dead from coronavirus, and Donald Trump will not say "I am sorry" or "I was wrong."

It is my mama's birthday. I planned to be with her today but I cannot. She is up north. I am down south. It is also Governor Tate Reeves's birthday. I wonder how he celebrates with the phantoms that hover around the Mississippi state flag I assume he keeps somewhere in his house.

DAY 9

113,774 Americans are dead from coronavirus. I wonder why so many white folks are contacting me today. Half are asking me if I'm okay. Half are telling me that they are ready to learn.

Fuck. Fuck.

I drive by the two massive Confederate monuments in Oxford. Black officers are guarding them both. I want to ask the brothers if they are humiliated guarding monuments that commemorate our destruction. When they start answering, or radioing for backup, I want to say, "Oh, one sec, bruhs."

Then I want to blast the first verse of "Fuck tha Police."

I imagine the brothers, parked in the shadows of the armed monuments, banging a beat on top of their cruisers, and all of us rapping "Fuck tha Police" until backup arrives.

When the white officer arrives, I imagine getting all bougie Black professor on them, explaining that white Mississippians cling to the confederacy not because they lost the Civil War, but because they cheated in a rigged battle against Black Mississippians. Their monuments are memorials of our suffering at the hands of folk who never had to pay, play, live, or fight fair.

But they already know that. Every Mississippian, whether they admit it or not, knows that.

What they don't know is that "Fuck tha Police" was one of our memorials, one of our most evocative monuments. And every member of N.W.A had roots in the South. I wanted to play it so badly as I watched that police precinct in Minneapolis burn and when Trump sicced his National Guard on peaceful protestors so he could get a photo Beelzebub would be jealous of.

I want to bump "Fuck tha Police" right now.

The existence of the song is proof that even if we could not bring as much material suffering to white folk as they did to us, we could memorialize and channel the spirits of those beaten and killed by nasty-ass cheaters. Mama's greatest worry is that I will be shot out of the sky by these cheaters. She is right. One day, I will not get up off the ground. Mama knows that in my dreams, we soar, bulletproof. And often, we crash. In my actual dreams, I run like Ahmaud. I shoot midrange jumpers like George. I heal like Breonna. I rap every lyric to "Fuck tha Police" in a Monte Carlo packed to the brim with them and Mignon and Tim and Henry and David fiending for new ways to love each other.

I fantasize about doing to white folks and their police what they do to us. And more than fantasize, I remember and relish publicly rapping words Grandmama could never whisper outside of her house.

But there is a way to commemorate our losses and our wins without humiliating queer folks, and subsequently morally debasing those of us who are not queer. Those who we seek to humiliate, we eventually seek to destroy.

And that first verse of "Fuck tha Police" does not fairly memorialize or commemorate the lives of queer folks. I had to stop rapping to it over two decades ago. I had to stop listening to it in 2015. As absurd as it sounds, the only thing harder than giving up "Fuck tha Police" was giving up lying to people I purported to love, giving up disordered eating, and giving up gambling.

Queer antagonism, like trans-antagonism, like anti-Blackness, is an addiction broken only by honest reckoning, consistent practice, and the welcoming of radical spirits.

Like most Mississippians, I am an addict. Like most Americans, I am a coward.

I wave at the Black officers guarding the Confederate monuments. They wave back. Adia Victoria's "And Then You Die" churns in the background, and I drive myself home.

Fuck. Fuck.

DAY 10

125,039 Americans are dead from coronavirus, and Donald Trump has not publicly worn a mask. The tired, tender nurse we pay to take care of my Grandmama has contracted coronavirus, and the Mississippi legislature—pressured by young people's power and the threat of losing money—has finally agreed to take down the Mississippi flag. Though it would have been politically devastating, Governor Tate Reeves could have stopped or slowed the flag from coming down.

I want to believe Tate did right for Mississippi because he remembers how wrong Black Mississippians have been done by white folks in Mississippi.

And/Yet/But/Somehow I cannot substantiate my belief.

DAY 11

126,929 Americans are dead from coronavirus and the virus is surging in Mississippi. Governor Tate Reeves vetoes a bill passed unanimously by the legislature that grants relief and forgiveness to residents in Jackson who cannot pay their water bill.

I tell myself it could all be so much worse.

DAY 12

128,761 Americans are dead from coronavirus, and according to civil rights icon Frankye Adams-Johnson, it doesn't matter if Governor Reeves or President Trump makes masks mandatory, says "I'm sorry" or "I was wrong."

The Awakening, she says, has begun.

The Mississippi flag no longer exists, and Ms. Frankye Adams-Johnson says that these times are biblical. Growing up in Jackson, Ms. Adams-Johnson was one of our civil rights superheroes. She grew up the child of sharecroppers right outside Jackson. Frankye marched with students from Brinkley High School to support protesters doing the lunch counter sit-ins downtown. Before they could get downtown, the high school students were arrested. Since there were too many students to fit in the paddy wagons, the police put the Black children in garbage trucks and took them to jail. An officer hit Frankye in her back with one of his rifles, then cocked the rifle and aimed it at her head. Frankye was seventeen years old the week Fannie Lou Hamer was nearly beaten to death in Winona and her youth leader, NAACP field secretary Medgar Evers, was assassinated in his Jackson driveway. Four years later, Frankye left Mississippi for New York.

I lather my hands in sanitizer before asking Frankye what she thinks of the young people who are risking it all for freedom during a pandemic, what the fall of the Mississippi flag means to her, and if it could all be so much worse.

"That rag sheet coming down won't erase history, but let me tell you something, Kiese, it sure helps release some of the pain I carried.

"When we sang 'We Shall Overcome' out in front of the Black Masonic temple, those crackers would be out there with that rag sheet talking about 'We shall keep the niggas down.'

"Mississippi sent me running for freedom in New York in 1967. My son was born there. Thirty-three years later, New York sent me running back to Mississippi to breathe. The young folks are experiencing what we experienced. They are awakening to the smells of freedom.

"It's an awakening. Call it what it is.

"They know this thing is rotten. They see that America, as we know it, is crumbling. You know who the hippies were? They were the master's children who'd turned on their parents. I don't care who you are, once you get that awakening, you will risk it all for freedom.

"The coronavirus is just terrible, but it has a biblicalness to it, you know? It's a rich time for writers to write. It's a rich time for awakenings. It's forced me to sit still and consider my own memories.

"The young people are working their way to the eye of the storm so we can all be free.

"They have given me so much joy. I worry though, about the battle scars, the trauma, the crumbs they will be given. You have to know yourself better than you know your enemy.

"That is what we didn't do.

"This is an awakening. But there are prices to be paid for awakening in this country. That's really all I can say."

I wipe the sweat from my neck, the tears from my eyes, and I lather my hands in sanitizer.

It could all be so much worse.

DAY 13

130,646 Americans are dead from coronavirus. Mississippi is surging, and President Donald Trump and Governor Tate Reeves have failed to make masks mandatory, or say, "I was wrong. I am sorry."

Here's what I want to believe:

Tate Reeves and all these white Mississippians who, just like us, immediately smell the difference between a collard and a turnip, who come from sharecroppers, who hear that bended brilliance in the blues, who hate the way Northerners use the South as a convenient shield against their trespasses, who feel the daily grace Black folks from the Deep South have offered white folks from the Deep South in the face of unrelenting humiliation, are being played by a devilish, desperate Northerner who has allowed his daddy issues—and inability to honestly revise—to ruin and eventually run his marriages, businesses, friendships, soul, and now his nation further into hell. There is a part of these white Southerners—like Tate Reeves, our white cousin by blood and culture, who refuses to heed the spirits of awakening—that is not evil or irrecoverable, but just easily seduced by power, inferiority complexes, and a longing to be accepted by a manipulative maniac who glided into the presidency with the cowardly winds of white American resentment at his back.

Here's what I know to be true:

Tate Reeves and most of these white men of Mississippi are no more regionalists, or lovers of Mississippi and the Deep

15

South, than Donald Trump is a patriot and lover of the United States of America. They are not haunted by phantoms. They are dedicated ghouls, spirit-repellant patriarchs who use each other and a muddled understanding of Jesus Christ to ensure the suffering of the most vulnerable. Abusive power tastes, touches, smells, sounds, and feels really good to gobblers of grace. They are not nineteen-year-old boys trying to decide between right and wrong; they are grown men who have chosen to model meanness for their posterity. They will torture and humiliate everyone close to them to maintain the power to abuse. They will never ever say or mean, I am sorry for making living harder than it needs to be. I am sorry for feeding off your humiliation. I am sorry for never confessing my actual sins to the world. I am sorry that your life means less to me than my ego. They will never say, I am sorry. They will only remind Americans and Southerners foolish enough to listen that it all could be so much worse.

The truth is, were it not for this awakening led by our young people and old spirits, they would be absolutely right.

DAY 14

131,870 Americans are dead from coronavirus, and I am turning in my piece to the editors at *Vanity Fair*. I know there is no incentive, credential, or subsidy for the spirits that guide us. Every dime of the money I make from this assignment will go to help residents of Jackson who cannot pay their water bills.

We are awakened, I want to believe.

Seventy-five miles from the armed Confederate statue in Oxford, Emmett Till's childish body was destroyed. Seventy miles from that armed Confederate statue, Fannie Lou Hamer was nearly beaten to death. A hundred and sixty miles from that armed Confederate statue, Medgar Evers was murdered as he entered his home. Eighty miles from that armed Confederate statue, Martin Luther King was murdered in Memphis.

I am wandering around the spiritual consequences of materially progressing at the expense of Black death. I want to be courageous. I wonder, though, when courage becomes contagious—when courage is credentialized, subsidized, and incentivized—if it is still courage at all.

Today, as I prepare to push send, and I lather my hands in sanitizer, it feels a bit too much like cowardice.

Maybe I'll wait to send tomorrow. Maybe I won't send at all.

The Lafayette County Board of Supervisors, a group of white men, unanimously vote to keep the armed Confederate monument in the middle of Oxford, the town where I live, teach, and write.

Humiliation.

The worst of white folk will not be persuaded; they can only be beaten. And when they are beaten, they fight more ferociously. They bruise us. They buy us. That is why we are so tired. That is why we are awakened. We are fighting an enemy we've shown exquisite grace, an enemy we've tried to educate, coddle, and outrun, an enemy that never tires of killing itself, just so it can watch us die.

Titillation.

I lather my hands in sanitizer and google gun shops in Lafayette County on my phone. I do not believe in guns. I do not believe in prisons. Yet I know I need a gun if I am to continue living alone in this Mississippi, American town.

I look at the grizzled cotton fields outside my truck window on Highway 6. I think of the underpaid essential workers in Oxford who call this town home. I want to ask, Where am I?

But I know.

This is not home.

If this is home, it is not healthy.

I do not want to humiliate. I do not want to be humiliated. I do not want to kill. I do not want to be killed. I want us to be free. I'm thinking about Malcolm's quip, in 1965, "Mississippi is anywhere south of the Canadian border."

Malcolm was so right.

Malcolm was so wrong.

Mississippi is here.

I reach out to Theron Wilkerson, one of the young Mississippians Frankye says has been awakened. Theron graduated from Jackson State and teaches African American studies at Murrah High School in Jackson. I ask Theron what he thinks of Frankye's proclamation and acceptance of awakenings.

"My daddy was forced to pledge allegiance to the Confederate rag in Carthage, Mississippi, from elementary until he received his diploma from Carthage High, way after this nation said the civil rights struggle was over.

"He was called a nigger on the same sidewalk he bagged groceries as a teenager, in the same town that his father's head was slammed with a hammer while taking a young Black mother and her newborn to the hospital, the same square county that routinely closed down business to pull a Black person out of jail to kill them on the courthouse lawn.

"It is no mistake to me this nation is the same for me as it is for my daddy and his daddy. My aunt and her peers flipped a mail truck over to protest the integration of the all Black O. E. Jordan High School. My father talks of destroying businesses on the square after viewing Roots in the segregated Carthage theater.

"My students talk of guns, power, and intervening on behalf of Black life and integrity. This nation's sin is its commitment to being the same, in any generation, as Black people are ushered into pent-up living and pent-down death."

Theron's students are right.

Theron is right.

Theron's father was right.

I must buy a gun if I continue to live in Oxford, Mississippi, so I cannot continue to live in Oxford, Mississippi, no more. It took way too much Black death to get here. And/Yet/But/Somehow here is where I'd love to live without guns, without prisons, without monuments of humiliation, without insistent desecration of indigenous life, without the undervalued expected sacrifice of essential workers, without unattended cowardice and addiction, without the worst of white folks.

Here is where I'd like to tenderly, honestly, radically, responsibly live and love with you.

And/Yet/But/Somehow here, will one day, be Mississippi.

WHAT I PLEDGE
ALLEGIANCE TO

There's a raggedy American flag hanging outside my house. I know I should take it down, but I'm afraid. For the past fifteen years, I lived in various apartments in Upstate New York. After accepting a new job at the University of Mississippi this summer, I moved into a university-owned house down the road from William Faulkner's home, Rowan Oak, in Oxford. Nothing about the new house or neighborhood surprised me more than the American and old Magnolia flags hanging in front of neighboring colonials, ranches, and bungalows.

I was born and raised in Jackson, just three hours south of Oxford, but I'd never seen a Magnolia flag before. The flag, which was the state's official banner from 1861 to 1865, has one white star in a square of blue in the left corner and one strip of red on the right. There is no prominent Confederate battle emblem in the corner like there is in our current state flag, which was adopted in 1894. There is simply a magnolia tree floating like a nappy green afro in the middle of white space.

On my first day in the neighborhood, all the green afro flags made me think my white neighbors were what my family called "them good white folk." Before I found out the Magnolia flag was actually Mississippi's flag of secession, I imagined these particular good white folk as courageous Mississippians wholly prepared to confront the layered traditions of white power and Black suffering that were violently stitched into our nation, our state, and today's prevailing Mississippi flag.

For me, the American flag is no better. Actually, it's far worse. It reminds me of what we Black folk have survived and witnessed at the hands of white folk hiding behind the American flag for centuries. Unlike the other flags in the neighborhood, the one flying outside my house might be the dustiest, most worn-out American flag I've seen in my life: the blue bleeds purple; the red fades pink; and the white wants desperately to be the color of bad banana pudding. There are two long rips on the top, and a more significant rip across the bottom bar. The flag rarely blows in the wind. Depending on the breeze, it leans slowly left or right, but mostly it just slumps, looking neither prideful nor ashamed.

I asked my mama what it would mean morally for an unapologetically ungrateful Black boy like me to let the flag fly. She told me it would mean bodily harm to take the flag down. But I swore against her wishes, promising to remove it the next weekend.

When the time came, I walked out on the porch, eyed the flag, smelled it, looked out at the neighborhood, but was ultimately too afraid to go through with it. Instead, I sat my big Black ass on the porch, sipped sweet tea that wasn't quite sweet enough, and watched white folk watch me watch them watch their property value plummet.

I waved, said "Hey there" and "All right now" like all petty Mississippians with good home training should. Sitting next to that flag in my new neighborhood, and hiding behind my Mason jar of tea and my college-issued MacBook, I felt like a wannabe Mississippi radical, a bougie Black sell-out, and a weak-kneed American wanderer hunting for a manageable fight to win outside. Inside, I was confused about where I'd been, where I was now, and who I could choose to be tomorrow. I was absolutely in need of someone to call my cowardice courage. I wondered if I'd chosen the wrong job, the wrong neighborhood, the wrong house, and the wrong state.

White American cowardice created Black intergenerational poverty. Black intergenerational poverty, among other things, was why I accepted a job and a subsidized home in Oxford, and not one in Jackson. The job in Oxford allowed me to take care of Grandmama the way she deserved to be taken care of. I am technically home, but I never associated home with this part of Mississippi, this many white people, or with America. Up north, in New York, I became a Black American. I came home to the Magnolia State, so I could be a Black Mississippian again.

. . . and to the Republic for which it stands . . .

As a Black child from Central Mississippi, I was encouraged by my mother and teachers to imitate the work of William Faulkner. Mama thought imitating Faulkner could protect me, ironically, from white men, white men's power, and all men's bullets. By the time I was fifteen, I'd read everything Faulkner had written. I knew *my* Faulkner like I knew *my* Ice Cube, *my Voltron, my* En Vogue, *my Good Times, my* banana-flavored Now and Laters. I loved knowing that Faulkner's literary virtuosity was inflected by his real and imagined experiences with Black Mississippians. Somewhere around eleventh grade, though, my body tired of imitating white writers who simply could not see, hear, love, or imagine Black folk as part of, or central to, their audience. I especially tired of white writers from Mississippi who, in my estimation, had enough deeply Southern home training and proximity to the ways of Black folk to know—and be—better.

When Callie Barr, a Black woman paid to clean up after the

Faulkner family, died in 1940, Faulkner delivered her eulogy. He said, "From her I learned to tell the truth, to refrain from waste, to be considerate of the weak and respectful to age. I saw fidelity to a family which was not hers, devotion and love for people she had not borne."

Of course, Black fidelity and devotion to white families that are not our own are a terrifying part of our story in this nation. And, of course, there was a lot Faulkner could not see in Callie Barr's work because white Americans, regardless of region, often have no clue about the shape of stories told and the depth of truth concealed under the timbre of our voices and the greased creases of our smiles. Still, I always believed that Faulkner's lessons learned from Callie Barr's supposed devotion and fidelity were foundational to any national or individual reckoning with American violence.

Tell the truth.
Refrain from waste.
Consider the weak.
Respect age.

Like my grandmother, Callie Barr spent most of her life cleaning up after white folk. Unlike Callie Barr, Grandmama never lived near the houses of the white families she took care of. The house where Callie Barr and her family lived is directly behind Faulkner's house. From the front of Barr's porch, one looks directly into the back of Faulkner's home. The porch of Barr's house, held up by weakened concrete, has one screen door in the middle and two windows on either side. The porch is worn and wobbly, just like the porch I grew up on in Forest, Mississippi. Unlike Callie Barr, my family did not have to look at anything white-owned from our porch. We did not own much, but we owned our shotgun house. We owned our porch.

24

We owned our small swath of land. We owned our garden, our Bibles, our books, our cinder blocks, our pecan trees, our sticker bushes.

And we owned our shotguns.

Those shotguns, and the stories surrounding those shotguns, always reminded me that my Black, deeply Southern family had neither devotion nor fidelity to white folk who could not see us. White folk who could not see us, sometimes led by police, often led by presidents and public policy, had no problems finding creative ways to encourage our death, destruction, and suffering. They could not see us, but they could always see our guns, whether the guns existed or not. These white folk had no devotion, no fidelity to us, and little love for themselves. Still, as good Christians, we often prayed for them and said things like, "Bless their heart, Lord, because they know not what they do." But if they ever knew not what they did on our property, near our porch, against the bodies of our family, they were going to get shot. Or shot at.

This is not a metaphor.

I've walked from my porch to Callie Barr's porch every day this month, looking and really listening for something. Last night, I think I heard it. After grown white men with no devotion or fidelity to Emmett Till tortured and shot him in the head seventy-five miles from where I live, Faulkner wrote, "If we in America have reached that point in our desperate culture when we must murder children, no matter for what reason or what color, we don't deserve to survive, and probably won't."

If William Faulkner loved, or at least imagined what Callie Barr saw happening to her children, what her children saw happening to her, or even what Barr and her children saw happening to the Faulkner family, he could never have said, "If we in America have reached that point in our desperate culture when we must murder children . . ." Faulkner would have known that you cannot love any child in the United States of America if you refuse to accept that this nation was born of a maniacal commitment to the death, destruction, and suffering of Black, brown, and indigenous children and a moral annihilation of white children. Faulkner would have accepted that there has never been a time in this desperate nation's history when American grown folk have refused to humiliate, abuse, and murder children.

This is not breaking news.

This is not a deep reading of our nation's habits.

This is not a progressive or remotely radical reading of our nation.

This is wholly descriptive of what I see from my new porch, under my old flag, in Oxford, Mississippi.

. . . one Nation under God, indivisible . . .

I spent the first weekend of this August down in New Orleans for my family reunion. I hadn't been to a big gathering with my father's side of my family in over two decades. When I was a teenager, there was a banquet, a cookout, and hot dogs were served, with maybe a game or two of kickball and spades long into the night. Now there were lip-sync contests, hashtags denoting our celebration, prizes, and conversations about Donald Trump.

Near the end of the banquet the first night, my older cousin Willie, who swears he invented everything from brake lights to wave brushes, did what he does every time he sees me. He started making presumed African tribal sounds, exaggerating the syllables in my name, and talking about how my father—who was a member of the Republic of New Afrika and was working in Zaire when I was born—should have sent a more American name over, like "Keith" or "Kevin." Willie didn't stop joking until I asked him to show me pictures of his new dog. When Willie pulled up a picture of his 180-pound mastiff on his phone, I asked him why he chose to keep such a huge dog inside. "You know I got felonies," he told me. "I can't carry guns no more."

Willie's words took me back to a few weeks earlier, when I interviewed my Grandmama for a new book project I was working on called *Heavy*. I asked her why she covered her face when she got nervous, and why she wore wigs all the time when her real hair was so beautiful.

"Choices," she told me. "Ain't nothing wrong with Black people on earth having choices. And I can't let no man, not even my grandbaby, choose my choice for me. These white folk don't think we deserve no choices, so we got to make healthy choices everywhere we can."

I thought about the tense and meat of stories on both sides of my family.

Always past.

Always present.

Always looking forward.

Always loving backward.

Always direct.

Always slant.

I wondered if the same discursive force that made our lies sound true, made us punctuate our truths with "Stop lying." How much of how we talked, listened, loved, and lied was American? How much was African? How much of it was the Mississippi in us?

Most of us had no idea where, specifically, in Africa we were from, but we knew we were the old and young descendants of African mothers and fathers and brothers and sisters brought to Mississippi to serve the economic and moral needs of powerful white folk. We knew we were not brought here to be equally protected under the law. We knew we were brought here to be subservient, to be hardworking, and to die.

In every pocket of the banquet hall, the reunion was packed with survivors: Black Mississippians who had shown up to reckon, dance, laugh, lie, and talk new memories into old bodies. I understood that night that these reunions were our attempt at reimagining American conceptions of family, freedom, and winning.

One of my father's brothers, Uncle Billy—a Vietnam veteran who did most of the planning for the reunion—wanted to talk politics before leaving the ballroom.

I told him that rich white folk got richer under President Obama and poor white folk got their jobs back and got more access to insurance than they ever had in their lives. "Obama is the best president white Americans will ever have," I told him. "He's the most white-folks-loving dude I ever seen. He act like he don't resent the terror they put him and his family through at all, and most of these white folks still hate the nigga."

My uncle stood there still without blinking. "Yeah, you're right," he finally said. "But if Obama is still talking, that means they ain't kill him. If they killed him, we likely to all be dead. You know how we do. Sound like a win to me."

I asked Uncle Billy if he was talking about metaphorical death.

"Symbols matter, nephew," he said. "Obama still being alive is a win for us and every nigga you know who got felonies. This America."

. . . with liberty and justice for all.

My first whupping in a Mississippi public school happened in third grade because I refused to stand and recite the Pledge. The American flag in our classroom hung right next to the state flag, its Confederate battle symbol always in eye's view. I didn't know much as a third grader, but I knew that I was from Jackson, home to thousands of Black American freedom fighters who never went abroad to fight. Those wonderful soldiers strategized, organized, and battled against the most patriotic, morally monstrous Americans on the face of Earth for me to be free. I still sit during the national anthem and the Pledge of Allegiance because they dared to love me and themselves when morally monstrous patriotic white folk with American flags, Confederate flags, and Mississippi State flags showed them that loving Black Americans was a murderous offense.

The same reason I choose not to stand for our pledge or anthem is strangely why I still haven't taken down the American flag flying outside my new house. It looks, to me at least, like every American flag on Earth should look: beat down, bleeding, fading, weak, tearing apart, barely held together, absolutely stanky, and self-aware.

American symbols and American choices matter. I have no idea how long I'll choose to live in this neighborhood. I have no idea what's going to happen to the neighborhood when or if I encourage more Black folks to move in if I stay. Every day that I live here, I will choose to fly the American flag out there now or some alternative. Some days I will choose to fly a red, black, and green freedom flag. Other days, I will choose to fly no flag at all. No matter what flag I choose to fly outside or inside of my house, many white Americans and white Mississippians will insist that *their* Black folk, Mexicans, and Muslims remain passive, patriotic, and grateful for the limited choices we've been *given*.

I am a Black Mississippian. I am a Black American. I pledge to never be passive, patriotic, or grateful in the face of American abuse. I pledge to always thoughtfully bite the self-righteous American hand that thinks it's feeding us. I pledge to perpetually reckon with the possibility that there will never be any liberty, peace, and justice for all unless we accept that America, like Mississippi, is not clean. Nor is it great. Nor is it innocent.

I pledge that white Mississippians and white Americans will never dictate who I choose to be or what symbols I choose to imbue with meaning. I pledge to not allow American ideals of patriotism and masculinity to make me hard, abusive, generic, and brittle. I pledge to messily love our people and myself better than I did yesterday. I pledge to be the kind of free that makes justly winning and gently losing possible. I pledge to never ever confuse cowardice with courage. I pledge allegiance to the Mississippi freedom fighters who made all my pledges possible. I pledge allegiance to the baby Mississippi liberation fighters coming next.

This is a pledge of allegiance to my United States of America, to my Mississippi. This is a pledge to my home.

Are y'all standing up?

DA ART OF STORYTELLIN'
(A PREQUEL)

From six in the morning until five in the afternoon, five days a week, for thirty years, my Grandmama Catherine's fingers, palms, and wrists wandered deep in the bellies of dead chickens. Grandmama was a buttonhole slicer at a chicken plant in Central Mississippi—her job was to slice the belly and pull out the guts of thousands of chickens a day. Grandmama got up every morning around 4:30 a.m. She took her bath, then prepared grits, smoked sausage, and pear preserves for us. After breakfast, Grandmama made me take a teaspoon of cod liver oil "for my vitamins," then she coated the area between her breasts in powder before putting on the clothes she had ironed the night before. I was ten, staying with Grandmama for the summer, and I remember marveling at her preparations and wondering why she got so fresh, so clean, just to leave the house and get dirty.

"There's layers to this," Grandmama often said, when describing her job to folks. She went into that plant every day, knowing it was a laboratory for racial and gendered terror. Still, she wanted to be the best at what she did—and not just the best buttonhole slicer in the plant, but the best, most stylized, most efficient worker in Mississippi. She understood that the audience for her work was not just her coworkers or her white male shift managers, but all the Southern Black women workers who had preceded her and, most important, all the Southern Black women workers coming next.

By the end of the day, when the two-tone blue Impala crept back into the driveway on the side of our shotgun house, I'd run out to welcome Grandmama home. "Hey baby," she'd say. "Let me wash this stank off my hands before I hug your neck."

This stank wasn't *that stink*. This stank was root and residue of Black Southern poverty, and devalued Black Southern labor, Black Southern excellence, Black Southern imagination, and Black Southern woman magic. This was the stank from whence Black Southern life, love, and labor came.

Even at ten years old, I understood that the presence and necessity of this stank dictated how Grandmama moved on Sundays. As the head of the usher board at Concord Baptist, she sometimes wore the all-white polyester uniform that all the other church ushers wore. On those Sundays, Grandmama was committed to out-freshing the other ushers by draping colorful pearls and fake gold around her neck, or stunting with some shiny shoes she'd gotten from my aunt Linda in Vegas. And Grandmama's outfits, when she wasn't wearing the stale usher board uniform, always had to be fresher this week than the week before.

She was committed to out-freshing herself, which meant that she was up late on Saturday nights, working like a wizard, taking pieces of this blouse from 1984 and sewing them into these dresses from 1969. Grandmama's primary audience on Sundays, her church sisters, looked with awe and envy at her outfits, inferring she had a fashion industry hookup from Atlanta, or a few secret revenue streams. Not so. This was just how Grandmama brought the stank of her work life into her spiritual communal life, in a way that I loved and laughed at as a kid.

I didn't fully understand or feel inspired by Grandmama's stank or freshness until years later, when I heard the albums *ATLiens* and *Aquemini* from those Georgia-based artists called OutKast.

• • •

One day near the beginning of my junior year in college, 1996, I had walked out of my dorm room in Oberlin, Ohio, heading to the gym, when I heard a new sound and a familiar voice blasting from the room of my friend John Norris, a Southern Black boy from Clarksville, Tennessee.

> . . . *my soliloquy may be hard for some to swallow but so is cod liver oil*

I went into John's room, wondering who was rapping about cod liver oil over reverbed bass, and asked him, "What the fuck is that?" It was "Wheelz of Steel," from *ATLiens*. Norris handed me the CD. The illustrated cover looked like a comic book, its heroes standing back-to-back in front of a mysterious four-armed force: Big Boi in a letterman's jacket with a Braves hat cocked to the right, and André in a green turban like something I'd only seen my Grandmama and Mama Lara rock. Big Boi's fingers were clenched, ready to fight. André's were spread, ready to conjure.

John and I listened to the record twice before I borrowed my friend's green Geo, drove to Elyria, and bought *ATLiens* for myself. Like *Soul Food* by Atlanta's Goodie Mob, another album I was wearing out at the time—their song "Thought Process," which featured André, had nudged me through the sadness of missing Mississippi a year earlier—*ATLiens* was unafraid of the revelatory dimensions of Black Southern life. Like *Soul Food*, *ATLiens* explored the inevitability of death and the possibility of new life, new movement, and new mojo.

But something was different.

I already knew OutKast; I loved their first album, *Southernplayalisticadillacmuzik*, in part because of the clever way they interpolated funk and soul into rap. *ATLiens*, however, sounded unlike anything I'd ever heard or imagined. The vocal tones were familiar, but the rhyme patterns, the composition, the production were equal parts red clay, thick buttery grits, and Mars. Nothing sounded like *ATLiens*. The album instantly changed not just my expectations of music, but my expectations of myself as a young Black Southern artist.

By then, I already knew I was going to be a writer. I had no idea if I would eat off what I wrote, but I knew I had to write to be a decent human being. I used ink and the page to probe and to remember through essays and sometimes through satire. I was imitating, and maybe interrogating, but I'm not sure that I had any idea of how to use words to imagine and really innovate. All my English teachers talked about the importance of finding "your voice." It always confused me because I knew we all had so many voices, so many audiences, and my teachers seemed only to really want the kind of voice that sat with its legs crossed, reading the *New York Times*. I didn't have to work to find that cross-legged voice—it was the one education necessitated I lead with.

What my English teachers didn't say was that literary voices aren't discovered fully formed. They aren't natural or organic. Literary voices are built and shaped—and not just by words, punctuation, and sentences, but by the author's intended audience and a composition's form. It was only after listening to *ATLiens*, discovering Toni Cade Bambara's Southern Collective of African-American Writers, and reading the work of my mama's former student, the hip-hop journalist Charlie Braxton, that I realized in order to get where I needed to go as a human being and an artist, in order to release my own spacey stank blues, I had to write fiction. Toni Cade, Charlie, Dre, and Big showed me it was possible to create and hear imaginary worlds wholly fertilized with "maybe," "if," and "probably."

I remember sitting in my dorm room under my huge Black

Lightning poster, next to my tiny picture of Grandmama. I was supposed to be doing a paper on "The Cask of Amontillado," but I was thinking about OutKast's "Wailin'." The song made me know that there was something to be gained, felt, and used in imitating sounds from whence we came, particularly in the minimal hook: the repeated moan of one about to wail. I'd heard that moan in the presence of older Southern Black folk my entire life, but I'd never heard it connecting two rhymed verses. Art couldn't get any fresher than that.

By the mid-nineties, hip-hop was an established art form, foregrounding a wide, historically neglected audience in completely new ways. Never had songs had so many words. Never had songs lacked melodies. Never had songs pushed against the notion of a hook repeated every forty-five seconds. Like a lot of Southern Black boys, I loved New York hip-hop, although I didn't feel loved or imagined by most of it.

When André said, "The South got something to say and that's all I got to say," at the Source Awards in 1995, I heard him saying that we were no longer going to artistically follow New York. Not because the artists of New York were wack, but because disregarding our particular stank in favor of a stink that didn't love or respect us was like taking a broken elevator down into artistic and spiritual death.

With OutKast, Dre and Big each carved out their own individual space, and along with sonic contrast—Big lyrically fought and André lyrically conjured—they gave us philosophical contrast. When Dre rapped, "No drugs or alcohol so I can get the signal clear as day," I remember folks suggesting there was a smidgen of shade being thrown on Big Boi, who on the same album rhymed, "I got an ounce of dank and a couple of dranks, so let's crank up this session." If there was ever shade between them back then, I got the sense they'd handle it like we Southern Black boys did: they'd wrassle it out, talk more shit, hug, and come back ready to out-fresh each other, along with every artist who'd come before them in the making of lyrical art.

OutKast created a different kind of stank, too: an urban Southern stank so familiar with and indebted to the gospel, blues, jazz, rock, and funk born in the rural Black South. And while they were lyrically competing against each other on track after track, together Big and Dre were united, railing and wailing against New York and standing up to a post–civil rights South chiding young Southern Black boys to pull up our pants and fight white supremacy with swords of respectability and narrow conceptions of excellence. *ATLiens* made me love being Black, Southern, celibate, sexy, awkward, free of drugs and alcohol, Grandmama's grandbaby, and cooler than a polar bear's toenails.

Right out of Oberlin, I earned a fellowship in the MFA program at Indiana University, to study fiction. For the first time in my life, I was thinking critically about narrative construction in everything from malt liquor commercials to the Bible. It was around that time that Lauryn Hill gave my generation an elixir to calm, compete with, and call out a culture insistent on coming up with new ways to devalue Black women. In *The Miseducation of Lauryn Hill*, I saw myself as the intimate partner doing wrong by Lauryn, and she made me consider how for all the differences between André and Big Boi, they shared in the same kind of misogynoir on their first two albums. *Miseducation* had me expecting a lot more from my male heroes. A month later, OutKast dropped *Aquemini*.

Deep into the album, the song "West Savannah" ends with a skit. We hear a young Black boy trying to impress his friend by calling a young Black girl on the phone, three-way. When the girl answers, we hear a mama, an auntie, or a Grandmama tell her to "get your ass in here." The girl tells the boy she has to go—and then the boy tells her that his friend wants some sex. The girl emphatically lets the boy know there is no way she's having sex with him, before hanging up in his face. This is where the next song, "Da Art of Storytellin' (Pt. 1)," begins.

In the first verse, Big rhymes about a sexual experience with a girl named Suzy Screw, during which he exchanges a CD and a poster for oral sex. In the second, André raps about Suzy's friend Sasha Thumper. As André's verse proceeds, he and Sasha are lying on their backs "staring at stars above / Talkin bout what we gonna be when we grow up." When Dre asks Sasha what she wants to be, Sasha Thumper responds, "Alive." The song ends with the news that Sasha Thumper has overdosed after partnering with a man who treats her wrong. Here was "another Black experience," as Dre would say to end another verse on the album.

Hip-hop has always embraced metafiction. In the next track—"Da Art of Storytellin' (Pt. 2)"—Big and Dre deliver a pair of verses about the last recording they'll ever create due to an environmental apocalypse. We've long had emcees rhyming about the potency of their own rhymes. But I have never heard a song attribute the end of the world to a rhyme. In the middle of Dre's verse, he nudges us to understand that there's something more happening in this song: "Hope I'm not over your head but if so you will catch on later."

Big Boi alludes to the Book of Revelation, mentions some ballers trying to unsuccessfully repent and make it to heaven, and then rhymes about getting his family and heading to the Dungeon, their basement studio in Atlanta—the listener can easily imagine it as a bunker—where he'll record one last song. The world is ending. He grabs the mic: ". . . The beat was very dirty and the vocals had distor-*tion*!" Of course, this ending describes the very track we're hearing, thus bringing the fictional apocalypse of the song into our real world.

I was reading Octavia Butler's *Kindred* at the time *Aquemini* came out. Steeped in all that stank, I conceived of a book within a book within a book, written by a young Southern Black girl whose parents disappear. "I'm a round runaway character" was the first sentence my narrator wrote. I decided that she would be an emcee, but I didn't know her name. I knew that she would tell the world that she was an ellipsis, a runaway ellipsis willing to do any and all things to stop her Black Southern community from being written off the face of the Earth. I scribbled these notes on the blank pages of *Kindred* while *Aquemini* kept playing in the background. By the time the song "Liberation" was done, *Long Division*, my first novel, had been born.

I thought about interviewing André and Big Boi for this piece. I was going to get them to spend the night at this huge house I'm staying in this year as the Writer in Residence at the University of Mississippi. I planned on inviting Grandmama, too. Between the four of us, I thought we could get to the bottom of some necessary stank, and maybe play a game of "Who's Fresher: Georgia vs. Mississippi." But the interviews fell through, and Grandmama refused to come up to Oxford because I'm the only Black person she knows here, and she tends to avoid places where she doesn't know many Black folks.

I kept imagining the meeting, though, and I thought a lot about what in the world I would say to Big Boi and André. As dope as they are, there's nothing I want to ask them about their art. I experienced it, and I'm thankful they extended the traditions and frequencies from whence we came. Honestly, the only thing I'd want to ask them would be about their Grandmamas. I'd want to know if their Grandmamas thought they were beautiful. I'd want to know how their Grandmamas wanted to be loved. I'd want to know how good they were at loving their Grandmamas on days when the world wasn't so kind.

The day that my Grandmama came home after work without the stank of chicken guts, powder, perfume, sweat, and Coca-Cola, I knew that her time at the plant was done. On that day—when her body wouldn't let her work anymore—I knew I'd spend the rest of my life trying to honor her and make a way for her to be as fresh and remembered as she wants to be.

Due to diabetes, Grandmama moves mostly in a wheelchair these days, but she's still the freshest person in my world. Visually, I'm not so fresh. I wear the same thing every day. But I am a Southern Black worker, committed to building stank-ass art rooted in honesty, will, and imagination.

This weekend, I'm going to drive down to Grandmama's house in Central Mississippi. I'm going to bring my computer. I'm going to ask her to sit next to me while I finish this essay about her artistic rituals of labor vis-à-vis OutKast. I'm going to play *ATLiens* and *Aquemini* on her couch while finishing the piece, and think of every conceivable way to thank her for her stank, and for her freshness. I'm going to tell Grandmama that because of her, I know what it's like to be loved responsibly. I'm going to tell her that her love helped me listen, remember, and imagine when I never wanted to listen, remember, or imagine again. I'm going to read the last paragraph of this piece to her, and when Grandmama hugs my neck, I'm going to tell her that when no one in the world believed I was a beautiful Southern Black boy, she believed. I'm going to tell Grandmama that her belief is the only reason I'm still alive, that belief in Black Southern love is why we work.

HOW THEY DO
IN OXFORD

"Born and raised where them Rebel flags hang from
them slaves . . ."

—Big K.R.I.T.

The sun is searing in Oxford, Mississippi. It's 11:05 a.m. on
the first Saturday of September. I'm standing for the national
anthem in Vaught-Hemingway Stadium. Though I left this state
twenty years ago, after being kicked out of college, Mississippi
is still home.

Today is officially White-Out Day at the University of Mississippi. I didn't know that. I'm wearing camouflage shorts,
a black Run DMC T-shirt, a faded red sweatshirt, black Adi-
das with fluorescent fat laces, and a Montgomery Biscuits hat
cocked to the left. Tens of thousands of young white folk are
wearing white polos, those Vineyard Vines club shorts, some
brown cowboy boots, and more long, flowing white dresses
than I've ever seen in my life.

I'm wondering who, and what, pays the price for ritualized
Southern comfort and uniformity. I can't take my eyes off the
backs of the student-athletes who play for the football program
at Mississippi. Their uniforms are a bright bloodred. Twenty of
the twenty-two starters look Black like me.

I'm also remembering the first real whupping I got in Mississippi, for wearing the wrong uniform.

I was nine years old. I needed an undershirt and a jersey for football practice. Mama was busy teaching at Jackson State, so she asked one of her grad students to take me shopping after school.

There were racks of blue-and-white Jackson State Tigers jerseys. All the other boys on my team wore those. Behind them were these discounted practice jerseys with the words "Ole Miss" and "SEC" in white cursive above the numbers.

I had no idea where "Ole Miss" was, what "SEC" meant, or that Mississippi was the last SEC football team to integrate, in 1972. As a Black boy from Jackson who lived and loved the game in the mid-eighties, college football began and ended for me with the historically Black universities in the SWAC.

Regardless of whether you lived in North or West Jackson, or whether your parents or grandparents were alums or employees of Jackson State, everyone used "we" to talk about the Tigers. And most of us had second-favorite teams of Alcorn, Southern, Mississippi Valley State, and Grambling.

We didn't know the names of the white schools in our state, or the names of any players who played for or against those teams other than Herschel Walker. Honestly, we didn't even know that some of those white schools had histories of refusing to recruit Black student athletes or play colleges and universities that did. We assumed so many legendary NFL players came from the SWAC because it had the greatest football tradition in our region. We knew that Jackie Slater, one of the most dominant offensive linemen in history, and Walter Payton, the best running back ever, played for Jackson State. We knew that Deacon Jones, one of the NFL's great defensive ends, and Jerry Rice, the most dominant college player in the country at the time, played for Mississippi Valley State. And everyone knew the Prancing J-Settes and the Sonic Boom of the South—Jackson State's trill dancers and thunderous band—put on the greatest halftime show on earth. If you didn't know any—or all—of that, we didn't really care to know you.

Mama had never let me pick out my own clothes before. On the left corner of the red Ole Miss jersey was the same symbol I'd seen on the top of the General Lee when Grandmama and I watched *The Dukes of Hazzard* on Friday nights. Next to the jerseys was a clearance rack of white T-shirts; on the front center of each stood what looked like an old, strange white pimp.

I'd never seen this pimp before. His long, white mustache dangled over his sunken cheeks. He wore a red suit, a huge red pimp hat. His right hand was behind his back. His left leg was slung jauntily over his right leg. His left hand held a red cane. The white pimp leaned on his cane, and he looked like a less husky version of Boss Hogg.

After practice, when Mama came to pick me up, she saw me in my new Ole Miss jersey. She walked onto the field, pinched the fat under my shoulder pads, and told me to get my ass in our Nova. Mama kept asking me questions about my uniform, but I couldn't understand why she was so mad.

Most of my childhood, Mama talked to me like an adult while disciplining me like a child, but this Ole Miss whupping and the accompanying staccato lesson were made for grown folk.

Mama explained to me how integral that Confederate flag on the jersey was to lynching, racial terror, and multigenerational Black poverty in Mississippi. She talked about how her mother, my Grandmama, worked fifteen hours a day sometimes for nothing but cornmeal under the watch of white families who flew the Confederate flag.

After the whupping, and the lesson, Mama laughed when I told her that Colonel Reb looked like an old white pimp.

"Pimps will never get love or attention in this house, Kie," she told me.

I asked Mama why any Black person would go to a school that glorified the Confederate flag.

"It's bigger than the Confederate flag," I remember Mama saying before we went to bed. "That flag just adds insult to injury."

I made the decision that night, as a third-grader, to never stand for the Pledge of Allegiance in any classroom that had in it the Mississippi state flag, the Confederate flag, or any other flag that devalued the Black lives and Black labor of my Mississippi family, and our people.

I kept that promise until today at my first University of Mississippi football game. After four strange weeks of living in Oxford, I'm wondering how many more promises I'm going to have broken.

Week 1

I first visited Oxford two years ago while on a book tour. Grandmama and Mama made me promise to leave town before the streetlights came on. When the creative writing program at the University of Mississippi selected me as this year's John and Renée Grisham Writer in Residence, my family expected the worst. I did, too.

Right now, I'm eating the best squash casserole I've eaten in my life, at a restaurant called Ajax Diner. Ajax is on the Courthouse Square, the economic and cultural center in Oxford. There are lots of white folk in the restaurant, and a number of illustrations of Ray Charles and other Black bluesmen on the wall. Twice I've heard, "We good, but we got to get a running game."

44

I keep hearing the names Nkemdiche and Laremy and Laquon and Fadol.

I'm a long way from Jackson, but the taste, the smell, and the rhythm of the names uttered in Ajax remind me of home. I have lived, taught, and written at a college in Upstate New York for the past fourteen years. In those fourteen years, I've never heard a white man say, "Collards pretty good tonight, ain't they?"

That's exactly what the white man at the table next to me keeps saying. I love that his color commentary is absent any linking verbs. I feel prideful that these Oxford white folk are eating our food and talking like us, even if they don't know it.

A few Black folk who work in the kitchen come out before I leave. We nod. I don't feel as good about them eating our food anymore.

On my way back to my car, I see my first two Confederate flags in Oxford. One is flowing in the bed of a pickup truck stopped near the courthouse. The other is rigged to the top of a silver Prius with a two-by-four and layers of duct tape. The Prius has a bumper sticker that says "HOTTY TODDY."

I look back at more white folks walking into Ajax. I look around the Square. I'm amazed, not by the swarms of white folk milling around but by how, in a county that's one-quarter Black, there can be so few Black folk downtown and so many of us at Wal-Mart. More than that, I'm wondering what it means for me to claim ownership over Black culture in Mississippi after having been away the same amount of time I lived there. The moral authority to critique Mississippi generally, and Oxford specifically, definitely belongs to someone. I'm not at all sure that someone is me.

Half a mile from home, I ask Google, "What in the world is a Hotty Toddy?"

Week 2

I wake up and read a letter published in the *Clarion-Ledger* from John Grisham, some workers from the university, and others protesting the Confederacy emblem on the state flag. They conclude: "It's simply not fair, or honorable, to ask Black Mississippians to attend schools, compete in athletic events, work in the public sector, serve in the National Guard and go about their normal lives with a state flag that glorifies a war fought to keep their own ancestors enslaved. It's time for Mississippi to fly a flag for all its people."

I reach out to Skipp Coon, one of my favorite artists and a native of Jackson, to see what he thinks of the recent conversation around the state flag, a conversation that has been reignited by the murders of nine Black folks in a Charleston AME church because they were Black.

"They can change all the flags they want," Coon tells me. "It's a false solution. It's also what Black people have always gotten. We asked for equality; we got integration. We asked for freedom; we got Reconstruction. They can change that flag and my material reality won't improve one bit."

I'm thinking about Skipp's use of the word "solution" and the letter's use of "fair" and "honorable." If changing the flag is a fair and honorable solution, I'm wondering what the writers of the letter assume the problem is.

Noel Didla, an English professor at Jackson State, introduced me to Skipp three years ago. In Jackson—and particularly at Jackson State—Noel, Skipp, and a host of other cultural workers are demanding new kinds of structural change. I ask Didla whether she agrees with Skipp.

"I believe symbols have lasting power to immortalize human stories," she answers. "But justice, equity, structural change, and truth should be the values on which undoing racism is founded. If not, the victory of bringing down the flag will remain an empty gesture rooted in white supremacy, coupled with white savior complexes. A principled and sustainable paradigm shift and nothing less is what we deserve."

I'm going to bed tonight in Oxford, Mississippi, wandering through the words of Skipp Coon, Noel Didla, and John Grisham. A principled and sustained paradigm shift that justly impacts the lives of Black Mississippians would be fair and honorable. But what do I say to people convinced that in spite of 40 percent of Black Mississippians living at or below the poverty line, a shameful approach to public education in Mississippi, and Mississippi being home to 246,000 children living in poverty as of 2013, my presence in Oxford as the Grisham Writer in Residence is proof that a principled and sustained paradigm shift has occurred already?

I'm wondering whether accepting the fellowship at the University of Mississippi was the fair and honorable thing to do.

Week 3

I'm on an elliptical machine at a gym in Oxford. I see a white man get out of a beige pickup truck and walk toward a Chinese restaurant. His gun is holstered on his left side.

Damn. This is how they do in Oxford?

While I'm looking at the armed man, a sweaty white guy walks up behind me. He sees me watching ESPN and asks who I think will start at quarterback this year, a player he calls "Machine Gun Kelly from Buffalo," another dude named Ryan Buchanan, or "the little Black guy, DeVante. DeVante Kincade."

I decide right there that I'm naming both the protagonist and the antagonist of my next novel DeVante Kincade.

When I get home, I reach out to my editor to make sure she sends me some tickets for the game Saturday. She says that she's hooking me up with a photographer from Atlanta named Daymon Gardner, who turns out to be a kind and curious white dude from Baton Rouge, and that we have tickets on the 50-yard line, two rows from the field.

I'm starting to get excited for football season at the University of Mississippi.

Week 4

The day before the game, Daymon and I meet with three women who work at the university's William Winter Institute for Racial Reconciliation. The institute is doing some of the most creative and necessary work around race in the country. Melody Frierson, a Black Korean woman, and two white women, April Grayson and Jennifer Stollman, sit down and talk about the challenges affecting the university, region, and state.

They tell me that the university is changing, maybe a bit too slowly sometimes, but that they're thankful that staff and administration are now aggressively asking for tools and the language to confront not just white supremacy but also homophobia and sexism. They highlight the crucial intersectional work being done at the Sarah Isom Center for Women and Gender Studies and the Southern Foodways Alliance.

"It doesn't mean that the Black students specifically don't suffer anymore, though," Jennifer tells me. "It does mean that they don't suffer as much as they did, and when they do suffer, they don't suffer alone. We're here. We're also seeing how the Black Lives Matter movement has positively impacted the work we do."

Melody laughs when I tell her that I'm going to the Grove the next day, before the game. The Grove is ten acres in the center of campus where thousands of students and alums drink, eat, and tailgate on football Saturdays. "I'm critical of everything this place was and can still be," she says. "But I still say to everyone in the country, 'You don't know how to tailgate like we do.' You'll see it tomorrow, Kiese. I hope you're ready to Grove."

I'm not ready to Grove.

Daymon and I leave the Winter Institute to go meet Sierra Mannie across campus. Sierra, a Black student from Canton, Mississippi, is a contributor to Time.com and the opinions editor at the *Daily Mississippian*, the school's student paper.

Near the end of our hourlong conversation, I tell her that people seem fixated on this idea of the university and the region changing, but that I'm curious whether Black students have been central to or on the periphery of that supposed change.

"This is my school," Sierra says, taking her hat off and revealing this unexpectedly fresh green hair. "I understood from the day I got here that this is college, not a Confederate day camp."

Damn. This is how they do in Oxford.

First Game Day: UT Martin

We're late. We get to the Grove around 9:30 a.m.

Tents filled with catered food are everywhere. I just passed some students making a pug do a keg stand next to a huge blowup of Colonel Reb.

"What's the angle for the story?" Daymon keeps asking me. "You think you want to talk to some people in their tents?"

I tell him that he can talk to people if he wants but that I'd rather just watch. I've never known happy things to happen to Black folk in Mississippi when asking questions of drunk white Mississippians proud to call themselves Rebels.

Daymon asks a group of older white folk whether he can

take a picture in their tent. The group has white candles, a blue Rebels helmet, and a huge silver vase filled with sunflowers sitting in between two mirroring pictures of Colonel Reb.

After Daymon takes a few pictures, one of the women asks what magazine he's with.

"ESPN," he tells them.

She curiously looks up at me.

"Oh, well, do y'all want something to eat?"

"Thanks," I tell her. "We good."

"You sure?" She hands us some bottled waters. "Here you go. Take these, at least. It's hot out here."

A band starts playing this mash-up of "Amazing Grace," "Swing Low, Sweet Chariot" and "Dixie," a Confederate anthem that originated during the minstrelsy era of the 1850s. I'm standing next to a middle-aged Black woman and Black man in matching jean shorts outfits. They look slightly less confused than I am.

The woman starts to clap near the end of the band's performance.

"You clapped for 'Dixie'?" the man asks.

"They play that one song at my church," she says.

"Right," he tells her. "But you clapped for 'Dixie,' though?"

"I'm here," she says, as the entire Grove erupts in a chant of "Hotty Toddy." "You asked me to come. I'm here."

Between the first play of the game, when Chad Kelly throws a 27-yard rope to Damore'ea Stringfellow, to early in the second quarter, when 296-pound defensive tackle Robert Nkemdiche tiptoes the sideline for a 31-yard touchdown, I fall in love with the Mississippi football team.

As impressive as the team's 76–3 victory is, watching the fair and honorable way the student athletes listen to each other, encourage each other, critique each other on the sideline—it makes me think I'm looking at a championship team.

I think I know what Hotty Toddy is.

Second Game Day: Fresno State

I'm watching in a Marriott bar outside of Detroit.

Mississippi is up by 50 in the fourth quarter when a short white man wearing a purple LSU hat sits down. "Leonard Fournette is old-school tough," he says. "He can win games by himself. We're a hard team to beat."

"We are too," I tell him, wearing the same good-luck uniform I wore to my first game in Oxford. "Chad Kelly, Jaylen Walton, that whole receiving corps, those jokers are the real deal. And our defense! As good as Fournette is, Nkemdiche is the best player in the country. Believe that. The only way we don't beat Alabama next week is if we run out of gas. I'm serious. We don't expect to lose."

We.

After the game, a 73–21 dismantling, my cellphone rings.

It's Grandmama telling me she's not coming to Oxford for Christmas. Grandmama has never been to Oxford. She just remembers how white folk went to war with themselves in 1962 over James Meredith's desire to learn in their school. Grandmama doesn't think James Meredith should have fought to learn next to folk morally beneath us. I tell her that I understand her point but that if he hadn't fought, maybe I wouldn't have even been selected for the fellowship.

"Those folk at that school won something when you decided to accept that fellowship thing," Grandmama says. "You know, I'm so glad you'll be closer to home, Kie, but you didn't win nothing."

Everyone in my family knows not to question Grandmama when she makes a proclamation, so I ask a related question. If there are so many parts of our state she's still afraid of traveling to, why did she stay in Mississippi in the 1950s, while hun-

51

dreds of our relatives left Mississippi for hopes of economic freedom in the Midwest?

"The land, Kie," Grandmama says. "We worked too hard on this land to run. Some of us, we believed the land would one day be free. That's all I can tell you."

I ask her whether the land is free now.

"These white folks ate good off of our work for long as I been alive," she says. "I'm tired, Kie, and I love my life, but I know what all we worked for. I know what we supposed to have. They know what we worked for, too. These folks, they know what they took."

Third Game Day: Alabama

I'm trying to sleep on a twin bed in a tiny boutique hotel in Brooklyn. I'm here for the Brooklyn Book Festival. I want to sleep in my own bed, in my own state.

I miss Oxford.

I just watched Mississippi beat Alabama in Tuscaloosa on ESPN. Professor Derrick Harriell, whose work at the University of Mississippi is another reason I accepted the residency in Oxford, messaged me throughout the game.

Derrick's loving words about the football team's will and work reminded me that Mississippi is the greatest and the most maligned state in this country because of the force, brilliance, and brutal imagination of its workers. Our literary workers, culinary workers, field workers, musical workers, educational workers, athletic workers, justice workers, and injustice workers have shaped national and global conceptions of what's possible.

Tomorrow, at the festival, I want to talk about why James Baldwin, a New Yorker born a few miles from my hotel and perhaps the greatest literary worker of the twentieth century, wrote, "I was going to be a writer, God, Satan and Mississippi notwithstanding."

Tonight, I'm thinking hard about the student athletes working on that field in Tuscaloosa.

I get out of bed to reread the letter Grisham and others wrote about the flag. I'm wondering how honorable it is to make money writing about the unpaid labor of student workers who come from families bearing the brunt of American racial terror. Instead of talking about how we can justly compensate these brilliant young workers, I feel compelled to write about whether they should perform under a humiliating state flag for a team called "Rebels."

Of course they shouldn't. Of course it's unfair, disrespectful, and anti-Black. But it's also a nearly insignificant part of what needs to change.

Last month, when asked in *Time* what it would take to finally have the state flag taken down, Grisham responded, "The flag will be changed, eventually. But it's Mississippi, and change is painfully slow."

Grisham is right, and he—as much as anyone in this country—knows that paradigm-shifting change will remain painfully impossible in Mississippi and the nation if we insist on targeting the symbolism of the insult while neglecting and often benefiting from the ongoing violence of the injuries. American—not simply Southern or Mississippian—investment in the pilfering of Black American life, labor, and liberty is the injury on which our nation feeds. It just is. We do not have a chance in hell of "fixing" or reforming that national truth with a local lie.

I learned that in Mississippi.

Week 7

I'm back in Oxford, sitting on the porch waiting for Grandmama to call and tell me whether she has reconsidered coming to Oxford for Christmas.

"The Ole Miss boys, they didn't give up when they could've," Grandmama says when she finally calls. "I thought they were close to running out of gas, Kie. You didn't tell me they had so many Black boys on the team. I prayed for every last one of those boys and their mamas last night. I prayed for the white ones, the Black ones, the Mexican ones if they on the team, too."

"Why?" I ask her.

"Because you live up there with them now."

I ask Grandmama if she might come up to Oxford if I get tickets to the next game, against Vanderbilt.

"Well." She pauses. "Well," she says again. "Kie. I can't bring a wheelchair to no ball game. The best seat I can get is probably right up under this TV. I reckon I'll watch the rest of Ole Miss games on TV this year, though. To tell you the truth, I hope Ole Miss win every game. I reckon they will, too."

"You do?" I ask her. "Why?"

"Because you live up there. And like I said, they didn't give up when they could have. They kept on going when that maroon-and-white team looked so strong. It's like they were playing on faith. Those boys worked hard and found a way to win that ball game. That's why," she says. "For all that those boys have been through, and all the work they put in up there in Oxford, they deserve to win it all. They really do deserve that."

HEY MAMA:
AN ESSAY IN EMAILS

Hey Mama, I'm feeling alone this morning up in New York. I miss Mississippi. I miss you. How you feeling?
Hey Kie, I'm tired. I'm wearing the pearl bracelet that you gave me. It is so beautiful. This morning I managed to get it locked alone. Did you hug yourself this morning?

Mama, you always say that. How am I supposed to hug myself?
You hug yourself by not allowing haters to distract you and by believing in yourself. You hug yourself by practicing the speech of respectability.

Oh, lord. Mama, some people theorize about the politics of respectability, but the crazy thing is how that's literally your theme music. How are you gonna sing your own theme music, though? I don't care about the speech of respectability. Respectability ain't got nothing to do with me.
Don't say "ain't got," Kie.

Or what?
Or nothing. Just don't say "ain't got."

Nah, I'm serious. Or what? I know the language, Mama. You know I know the language. I know the rules. I know how to

break and bend the rules, too. Plus, who would win in a contest between "doesn't have" and "ain't got"?
It depends on the judges.

Mama, how have we been having the same conversation about language for thirty years?
You are a grown man, but you're still a Black boy from Mississippi to people that want to hurt you. Speaking and writing in a respectable way is just one small way to protect yourself. How do you not understand this?

I have pictures of the look on my Grandmama's face the first time she held my books. Grandmama smiled until she cried. I haven't had those kinds of moments with Mama. I do know that she wishes I'd share less in my work and that I'd never write anything with the words "nigga" and "ain't got" in it. I want to write this new book about us, really about us, but I'm scared. Not sure how to write honestly where we've been. Mama has been sending me titles for the books she wants me to write for over twenty years. The last title she sent me was At My Age. *I think Mama knew I'd write something, but I don't think she imagined, or wanted, my first, second, fifth, or tenth book to be what* my work *became.*

Hiding won't protect us.
I'm not talking about hiding. Public and private are different words for a reason. If you had children, I bet you wouldn't talk or write the way you do. Maybe you should refrain from that Twitter and Facebook for a few weeks.

I don't even really do Twitter, Mama. If people follow me, I follow them, and if they read my stuff, I tell them thank you. What do you even know about Twitter?

My friends tell me you write crazy talk on that Facebook, and that Twitter. I hear something in your voice that's worrying me. Whenever I hear this, you end up doing something destructive. Are you okay? Have you written about Jordan Davis yet?

Mama. Both of my books are about Jordan Davis's life and death. Wow. I've been thinking about Obama's My Brother's Keeper initiative.
What have you been thinking?

I've been thinking too much. If the president isn't willing to even say the words "Black love" or "white supremacy" or "patriarchy," he can be a Black boy's keeper, but he can't be an honest lover of Black boys. They're trying to fix Black boys on the cheap, without reckoning with white supremacy. You fix a "what." You don't fix a "whom." What really needs fixing? It's dishonest and violent to focus on Black boys when Black girls are catching hell from everything under the sun, and catching hell from Black boys and Black men. Don't get me started. I get the restraints Obama is under. I get that his job is to lie to a nation of liars. But don't bring Black boys up on stage and lie to them in front of the world. In front of Bill O'Reilly? I hate when folks use us as props. And then they had the little brothers dressed in the same outfits. It was so shameful. I'm wondering, Do you think the nation or our state has ever, or will ever, loudly and lovingly focus on the lives of Black girls and Black women?
It hasn't. And it won't. Black girls and Black women don't really buy the president anything in this country, though we supported him with a higher percentage than any other group in both of his elections. But do we really want Black girls added to what you called "cheap initiatives"? The state generally works to dismantle our right to dignity. That work of valuing our lives, sadly, has always, and will always, be done on the local level.

Actually, I woke up this morning thinking about Fannie Lou Hamer and Margaret Walker Alexander. I don't know why, but thinking about them, and your relationship to them, and the lives they lived in Mississippi, just made me so sad. Usually, thinking about them is a way of hugging myself, like you say. But today, I just feel the worst part of the weight they experienced as Black women activists and artists living in Mississippi. I learned about Mrs. Hamer from Leslie. Leslie had been a young student activist and had worked with the Mississippi Freedom Democratic Party and Mrs. Hamer. I learned how she embraced young people and the SNCC folk who recruited her in Indianola, and how she joined the movement realizing that she would be kicked off the plantation and left homeless. I hurt for her all over again when I read and reread how she was sterilized and beaten in Winona, and how she did not have good healthcare during her bout with cancer. Even after all she did for our state, she died painfully, poor and penniless. She matters to me even now because she fought to help the nation and our state get closer to its creed. You love Mrs. Hamer as well. Why is that?

I didn't have a choice. You made me love her, Mama. I felt loved by Fannie Lou Hamer the first time you made me watch this documentary about the Mississippi Freedom Democratic Party. I didn't have the words back then, but I just felt so loved when she said, "White Americans today don't know what in the world to do because when they put us behind them, that's where they made their mistake. . . . They put us behind them, and we watched every move they made." She made me believe in time travel and believe I was a part of a team of time travelers. Wait, Mama. Can you tell me more about your relationship with Margaret Walker Alexander? I remember you always being at her house. She was the first real Black writer I ever met. Did she ever talk about her time in the Black arts movement?

Margaret was a very complex woman. My best memories of Margaret are visits to her home, where she invited me to help her sort out materials for a book she wanted to write on Aaron Henry. I had taught her son Sigmund and knew her daughter-in-law and her elder son. So, I knew her well and enjoyed her stories. She, like you, was not fond of flying. Margaret and Eudora Welty were both Jacksonians, and I always had the sense that Welty got the better end of the royalties and national attention because she was white. I often wondered how Margaret and Welty might have fared as friends and why the gulf was impermeable.

Yeah, for a long time, I hated on Eudora Welty's narrative abilities because my teachers made us read her every year from seventh to twelfth grade, and I knew that Ms. Alexander's *Jubilee* and "For My People" were way better or at least as good as anything Ms. Welty did. Ms. Welty was dope. She was. She layered her stories, and did white Southern characterization better than almost anyone ever. But Mississippi is the home of the best sentence creators in the world. How come Ms. Welty was the one who got all the shine when I was in school? Plus, I hated how it sounded when she said "nigra" on tape. What's a "nigra"? A mix between a "nigga" and a piece of okra?

You are so crazy.

I'm a crazy nigra. My irrational hate of Ms. Welty's work eased by the time I went to college. But then one of my teachers worked with Ms. Welty, and this teacher accused me of plagiarizing because I used the word "ambivalent." It was the second week of class, and this woman literally said, "Ambivalent isn't a word I can see you using." When I went back to Mill-

saps to give a talk last year, I let her know that I was a better writer than her and she should be happy that I'm not ambivalent about talking to her wack ass.
You are so crazy.

Maybe. People on Facebook keep asking me what you think about Chokwe's death. I say that you're not ready to talk about it. I know that he meant so much to you and my father.
Have you talked to your father since Chokwe's passing? My first date with your father was to the Republic of New Afrika House on the corner of Lynch and Dalton streets. I was eighteen. Across the street was my favorite chili dog restaurant, The Penguin. In any case, Chokwe was much respected and admired by your father. I was very new to the conversation but found it interesting. Inside the RNA House were tons of books, the smell of incense that I mistook for the smell of weed, and lots of candles. Later I would meet Chokwe and the late Imari Obadele. I actually adored Imari. The police raided the House around midnight and our date was over. Chokwe loved the name that we gave you. "Kiese Makeba." We were so proud of that name. Chokwe spent his entire life using his skills to help dispossessed Black people in the South and the Midwest. . . .

Black folks loving Black folks in the south causes so much literal terrorism, yet Black love is also the only place we could go to soothe the terror. Mama placed Mayor Chokwe Lumumba in a larger context of complicated freedom fighters committed to freeing the land. This was a part of our conversation that my mother made me promise not to share with the world.

. . . I do not want to believe that there was any foul play in Chokwe's death, Kie. The possibility of that so disturbs me— to the point of having an existential crisis. All my life I have believed that people are basically good—this would change that belief.

Mama, I'm not sure how you can believe that people are basically good after all that we've seen. Remember when we were playing by Calloway and we ran after that man who just started destroying that woman's face?
I do not want to talk about that, Kie. I still see that girl's bloodied face and hear the sound of that man punching her. I think we would have killed him if we caught him.

No question. So how can you still believe people are basically good?
What's the alternative, Kie?

The alternative is to accept that white supremacy and cis-heteropatriarchy don't want us to ritualize the work of loving each other, which means white supremacy and cis-heteropatriarchy literally want us dead. We ain't dead yet. We ain't even got good at really loving each other and we still ain't dead yet. So we just have to get better at the hard work of loving each other. That means loving at home, loving policy, loving institutions, loving economically, all that. Wait, would you raise a girl or boy in Mississippi or the South if you could do it again?
If I had to raise a child now—no matter the gender—I would probably not choose Mississippi. There's so much love and history of Black excellence in our state, but the state's structural commitment to Black death is unparalleled.

But if that's true, why did you stay there so long?
I stayed there so long precisely because of the state's commitment to Black death and my commitment to my students. I

loved my students because my teachers had loved and believed in me. Like you, I was only a few years older than my first class of students, so I was committed to advancing their life chances. I needed to do my part to ensure their sure-footedness in the next leg of their journey, whether they stayed in Mississippi or left.

What would you think if I moved back to Mississippi next year to teach and learn?
I do not favor this move. Would you be moving without a job? Would you be moving for reasons that could easily change? What's happening with you? Has Vassar asked you to leave? Is this your decision? Why?

Damn, Mama. Why you trippin'? I'm just asking what you'd think of my moving back home to live and work.
And I'm asking you why you're considering that after all you've been through.

Oh, boy. Okay, next question. Sometimes I wonder if I really had a chance to be anything other than a teacher, a student, and a writer after being conceived, born, and raised on a college campus. When I watched you teach, I didn't think about how much love students share with you, or how you can really damage them if you're not attentive, honest, and deliberate. I've been my best self when teaching and learning from students. There's so much I didn't think about regarding the relationships with students and teachers when I watched you. I remember kids asking me why your students lived with us sometimes. And I never thought the answer was because you loved them. But that really was the answer.
They loved me, Kie.

When I was a kid, I thought you loved them more than you loved me. But after a while, I didn't care. I understood that you were changing the world, and being changed, one student at a time.
That's true.

Let me ask you this: Would you whip me as much as you did if you could do it over again? No beef. Just asking.
I did not want you to destroy your life chances and I did not want racism to destroy you. That's why I whipped you so much. As a child, you had enormous stubbornness, anger, and rage. And while you were able to channel it through sports and writing, it was never far from the surface. Sometimes I wonder if much has changed with you. I tried to establish rules, and when talking did not help, I lost patience. I was nineteen when I was pregnant with you. I am sorry, Kie. Please forgive me.

I get all of that, Mama. I really do. You were a baby with a baby. I remember men constantly asking me for my "sister's digits" when we were in the mall. That shit made me so mad. Then you add on living in Mississippi. And being in academia, with all its crazy-making. And all the men who were trying to eat your heart meat. I get it. I'm telling you I get it. Do you think being a young Black woman in Mississippi with a child impacted your relationship to money?
I never had a job or a bank account as a young woman and probably never learned to value money the way I should have. In any case, I earned seventeen thousand dollars the year I began work at Jackson State. I immediately enrolled you in Christ the King. I think your father contributed two hundred and fifty dollars a month. After rent, your schooling, food, clothing, and utilities,

there was very little left for purchases other than books. I feel like I never had enough money to give, spend, or save.

I hear you. Can you tell me why you want to be a grandmother so badly?
Kie, sometimes I think you're afraid to have kids or get married because of mistakes your parents made. Is that true?

I wasn't ready to answer that question honestly. Family, community, and my grandmother are central in nearly everything I've ever created, but there are huge gaps in my fiction and nonfiction where textured mothers, fathers, and partners are supposed to be. There's the thinnest line between parental terror, parental shame, and parental intimacy, and I'm trying to understand how my parents drew and toed that line, and what the consequences are for children when those lines blur. I guess I'm mostly reckoning with whether I have the imagination and will to draw something other than scary thin lines for my children, and my partner. Scary thin lines poke. And people aren't ideas. People bleed. Then they scar. I don't want to be an abusive parent or partner. I'm not sure people should have kids if they're unsure whether they themselves are really worthy of love. Anyway, I'm working on it.

Maybe.
If you have kids, especially if you move back home, protect my grandchildren and teach them that life is a series of choices, and whatever we choose, we lose something. Make sure you have children with a woman you're madly in love with. Don't ever be a whoremonger. Teach my grandchildren to read, write, sing, and dance. They will probably have a good set of windpipes and great hand-eye coordination. They will also be very beautiful. Teach them what you value most—the power of dig-

nity and the complexity of love. Don't be afraid that you'll mess up or that they won't love you. Loving you is not hard. I wish I showed you that more.

I hear you, Mama. Okay, so are you gonna let me run all that other stuff you said I couldn't run?
No, I'm not. Why would you want strangers without our best interest at heart to see that?

Thanks for talking to me, Mama.
Thank you for talking to me.

Ain't got. Ain't got. Ain't got.
You are so hardheaded.

I love you, Mama.
I love you, Kie.

ECHO: MYCHAL, DARNELL, KIESE, KAI, AND MARLON

Peace Fam,

I'm just waking up on the anniversary of Malcolm X's assassination, the birthday of Nina Simone, and I feel small. I'm not comparing my life's accomplishments to either of them. I've learned enough to stop making that mistake. But I still compare myself to who I think I should be by now and the vision is incomplete.

I'm twenty-six now, and for the first time I feel comfortable enough calling myself a man, but can't help thinking of all the years I was confused about what that meant. I got into an argument with my pops when I was twenty-one, I can't remember what it was about, and he asked me, "Do you think you're a man now?" and through my whimpering I admitted, "No." I was answering on his terms. I was still in school. I didn't have any real bills, or a job, a place of my own . . . you know, man shit. And the longer I went without any of those things, the less I felt like I would ever become a man, with his eyes constantly on me, asking without saying, "When are you going to get it together?"

Hell if I knew. I had this vague idea about being a writer because that's the only skill I had (still is, but don't sleep on my cookie-baking abilities), with no earthly idea of how to make that happen. The days I didn't have an appointment with my therapist I spent in bed watching cable news and writing really horrible poetry. When I wasn't having a panic attack, I was thinking about the last panic attack and anticipating the next. All the while, the disappointment in my pops's eyes was palpable. He was wondering where he went wrong, and I was being crippled by the thought that I'd never be enough of a man to make him proud.

I'm trying to pinpoint the moment I stopped worrying and started living. I can't, really. I still worry, but it doesn't overwhelm me. Something broke along the way and I'm free. I can call myself a man now because I love and feel loved. And for me that's all it takes.

I think of all the time I wasted not knowing that and I feel small. I'm looking at my text messages now. Yesterday, my pops told me he loved me. I'm twenty-six, he'll be fifty-two soon, and I think he's told me he loves me more in the last year or so than during the entire rest of my life. I can't help but think of what we missed.

I wish I had that time back. I wish I knew my worth a long time ago. But here I am.

With love,
Mychal Denzel Smith

Dear Mychal,

I cannot help but think that this performance called "living" is the most radical act that we Black men can commit ourselves to.

Unlike you, I did not (and still do not) spend a lot of time in therapy, even though I graduated with a master's degree in clinical counseling, and even though I knew, the first time that I tried to end my life, that I needed help more than the helping profession needed me. But like you, I spent a lot of time in bed during my early twenties. Dreams, when I could actually sleep, were a welcome escape from . . .

Life: Staying awake, staying alive, meant that I needed to figure out how the hell I would persuade other folks in my life that I was straight and, therefore, acceptable and honorable as a Black man. Fuck trying to live for my father, who didn't know that I wanted to die . . . who didn't know what under-grad institution I was in at the time . . . who didn't really know me . . . probably because he, too, was most likely trying just as hard as me to live. Nah, I was too worried about living for the Father, that other God, who apparently hated me enough to let me burn eternally in hell because I preferred to love other men. Ain't that torture? But my Black mama knew best. She told me that I should not keep anyone in my life who refused to love me.

Yet, if I were to adhere to my mom's advice, I would have had to drop out of school years ago (since a lot of folks in our inequitable educational system refuse to love us), quit engaging public health offices (because I walked in as a human in need of medical services and walked out as a patient whose subjective world was made invisible by research lingo: "MSM," otherwise known as "men who have sex with men"), sleep in my bed all damn day (knowing it is more likely that I would be stopped by police when walking to the store in Camden or Bed-Stuy while rocking a fitted cap and carrying books than my white male neighbors would be while walking around in ski masks in the middle of summer and dropping a dime bag on the ground in front of a walking police and his dog) . . .

See, this thing that we call "living" is as revolutionary as Black gay Joseph Beam's call for Black men to love other Black men, precisely because it is a command for us to counteract the very processes of annihilation that structural racism and patri-archy have taught us to love and replicate. We are experts in the art of killing because we know what it is like to be killed, maligned, have our spirits deadened, our bodies pillaged. We know. But we cannot demonstrate our knowledge by rearticulating the very violences that have been used to murder us.

I am a Black man and I am still alive. And, yes, I am a revolutionary, because I daily choose to live! But I am a Black man whose Black mama's body and spirit were terrorized by another Black man's hands and words. *Sexism and patriarchy are not part of the revolution.* I am a gender-maneuvering gay Black man whose spirit was terrorized by other straight Black men. *Heterosexism and heteronormativity are not a part of our revolution.* I am a Black man who has ignored the plights of so many of my brothers. *Separation because of difference and elitism based on class are not a part of the revolution.* Indeed, my living is your living, is your father's living, is my father's living, is my mother's living, is the stranger's living, and it is the revolution.

If God needs to condemn anything to hell, it ought to be the idea of social death. Every day we commit an act of revolution, an act of treason, against a system that was never meant to guarantee our survival.

More love,
Darnell Moore

Dear Darnell and Mychal,

Your letter to Mychal took me back to a Baldwin essay. In "Alas, Poor Richard," an essay that I still find a bit too brutalizing of Richard Wright, Baldwin wrote, "Negroes know about each other what can here be called family secrets, and this means that one Negro, if he wishes can 'knock' the other's 'hustle,' can give his game away."

Long before I read the Baldwin essay, and long before I remember Tupac Shakur, Nasir Jones, and Dwayne Carter giving lessons on how our love for brothers and riches was always more important than our love of Black women, I understood the gendered expectation of that hustle Baldwin writes about. No matter what another Black man I cared for did to a woman or a group of women or his male partner, I was never to call him out or tell other people about his game.

I want to change.

The Black man with whom I spent most of my life was not my father. This Black man had an aneurysm two weeks ago. Bad books would call this Black man "a father figure." (Like both of you, I try not to write bad books.) This Black man never told me he loved me. He never called me his son. He never told me I could be better. And, truth be told, I never wanted or needed him to do any of that shit. I liked him and I think he liked me.

That was enough.

Femiphobic diatribes and other bad books have gassed us with this idea that Black boys need the presence of Black father figures in our lives. I'm sure I'm not the only Black boy who realized a long time ago that my mother and her mother and her mother's mother needed loving, generous partners far more than I needed a present father.

Mama disciplined me. She loved me.

Aunt Sue prayed for me. She loved me.

Grandmama worked for me. She loved me.

That's why I made it through the late eighties and nineties. That is why I am alive. Black children need waves of present, multifaceted love, not simply present fathers.

Anyway, I believed this Black man loved how my mother made him feel . . . until he didn't. He loved her mind . . . until he didn't. He loved her persistence . . . until he didn't. I know my mother loved him, and loved what he tried to teach me. This Black man tried to teach me that white folks were never

71

to be emulated, that Black life came from Black farmers, and that a love of Black people necessitated a love of the land we toiled, picked, and raked. This Black man tried to teach me to own myself, Darnell, to never work for a white man. I learned later that owning myself was very different and, really, a lot easier than loving myself.

This Black man physically and emotionally brutalized my mother. I fought him for that, but I never told anyone. My mother broke up fights between us. I wiped her tears, put ice on her swollen eyes and split lips, and never ever talked about what this man did to her. This Black man was respected in our community, and I could have knocked his hustle by telling the truth to him, to my mother, or to anyone who knew us, but I never did.

I knew not to. I knew that telling was not only spreading my mama's business; it was also a form of knocking this Black man's hustle. And that, I believed, was not how one Black man should love another.

Darnell, your letter really made me think about how not knocking another brother's hustle was seen as Black men loving Black men. Your letter reminds me that any love that necessitates deception is not love. It doesn't matter if that supposed love is institutional or personal. Your letter reminds me that when you don't let love breathe, you can't be surprised when you and those around you suffocate. We Black men have suffocated our partners and ourselves for a long, long time. We Black men have been suffocating. For a long, long time. And I'd like it to stop. I want to work on loving you and Mychal and Kai and Marlon, and I want all of you to work on loving me. Please knock my hustle, Darnell. Please remain my friend when I knock yours. Please love me, brother, and encourage me to be a healthy part of healthy relationships, no matter what. There is no proof that most of this nation has ever really wanted us to live with dignity and equal access to healthy choices, so we have to take better care of ourselves. We have to change.

I am regretful and ready to be better at love.

I need your help,
Kiese Laymon

Dear Kiese, Darnell, and Mychal,

I THANK you.

I THANK you for being vulnerable. I thank you for going deep and being unafraid to share that with me. All of these letters made me ask myself a question that I ponder a lot: What do we do with the scars, those of us who did not die, but still aren't free? We struggle. We fight. We make a way out of no way. Every day we prove that the impossible is possible just by living.

You are right, Mychal, trading worry for living, for being, is freedom—it's about being present.

You are right, Darnell, loving ourselves is a revolutionary act—we have to practice because the preachers and their Bibles don't always tell us so.

You are right, Kiese, love can't be attained through ownership—love is a relationship that must be cultivated through honesty. The truth can hurt, but a lie will never set you free. I, like you, choose truth. Please love me enough to tell me the truth.

Can we heal ourselves?

Yes! And we are modeling that process here. It takes self-reflection.

These days when I look in the mirror, I see change. I see my hips narrowing. I see my jawline sharpening. I see the physical markers of Black manhood etch a divine design upon my body, and I feel pretty.

But I wasn't born this way. I was born a Black girl and I grew up into a Black woman. I was once a queer hippie kid searching for peace in a New England boarding school because home could no longer hold me. I was once a masculine-identified lesbian, a femme-loving stud who was afraid to love other masculine folk—I was never told it was okay for us to love one another and that our love was valuable, too. And today I write this as a Black transman, queer boi, lover of love. I chose this life.

But what do we do with the scars? I have scars. Visible scars from falling as a kid. Visible scars from nights of self-inflicted cutting in high school. Visible scars from my recent double mastectomy. Those scars are easier for me to deal with because I know where to find them. I know what might irritate the recent scars on my chest. But what of the scars that you can't see?

You ever go so deep and remember the things you didn't know you were reminding yourself to forget?

Sadness. It haunts me. It sits on me sometimes and I wish I could move it, transition it.

I only recently learned that the sadness I carry is not just my own. It was inherited. Both my mother and father struggle with depression, but no one ever told me. I thought I was alone, and we still struggle to talk about it—how things from way back when still hurt us. And how we never got to take a break after losing so much.

Once I asked my mother about crack. I asked her about my dad. I asked her how she loved him. I asked her why she made me love him even though he hurt us over and over.

She told me she felt shame. She told me that I was the only one she could talk to because everyone thought she was crazy to stay, but she loved him. That he was her husband and my father, and she knew his heart. Crack changed him. Crack destroyed so many Black love stories.

She told me that it was only in the last couple of years that she had stopped sleeping with her purse under her pillow for fear of having it stolen. She hasn't been with my dad in more than six years. Scars . . .

If you cared about it, you had better lock it up in the back room. I remember the frustration of forgetting, forgetting that nothing was safe unless you locked it away. I remember when something of my big brother's got stolen. I remember how angry he was. I remember how guilty I felt because it was my father who was the addict, not my big brother's father.

I remember God. God and my mother were the only people I was allowed to talk to. We kept secrets from the outside world—we built our own. But we needed more. We couldn't save my dad. I couldn't save my mother. I learned the most radical thing I could do was figure out how to save myself. We all have to save ourselves. We all have to find our way toward healing and forgiveness. And it is a long road.

I am a Black transman who loves men and women. I am a man who is just now learning to love my femininity. I was a girl named Kiana once. She survived a summer of sexual abuse when she was eight. When she told the truth, there was no counseling. There was no processing, only a *fast girl* who needed to be watched closely. I prayed to God for forgiveness. Guilt hurt, and I started getting migraines. I moved with guilt in my heart, guilt as my center. I didn't want to be bad, but I felt bad. I carried guilt when I left my mother with my father, but it was the only way I could get free. I had to leave.

I am Kai. I had to leave. I had to move into this new body.

Sometimes we don't get what we deserve because we don't know our own value.

WE deserve great love, laughter, poetry, sweetness, sunshine, and smiles.

WE deserve true love, open and honest.

We deserve healthy love—love, a home where you don't have to hide what is most valuable in order to keep it.

I write with love for you, brothers, the agape kind.

Kai M. Green

Dear Kai, Kiese, Darnell, and Mychal,

Damn, you guys are bringing up some things that are making me go deeper than I want to go. Just two months ago, I was finally able to voluntarily move out of my parents' house. FYI: I said voluntarily because I spent a decade in what some of my brothers call Mr. Gilmore's house, aka the big house. I've been in prison for the last ten years of my life.

I'm Black and from Brooklyn, so my spending time in Mr. Gilmore's house ain't no thing nowadays. Y'all know the stats about Black men in prison, so I will spare the choir the gospel. But, man that ain't the half of it all. I got people telling me that I need to see a quack because they think I'm emotionless . . . gotta admit, I think I am, too. I mean, I care about a whole lot of people and things and issues. In fact, my whole life is dedicated to caring. That's why I do the work that I do, mentoring and nurturing the hood to be safer and so on. But, brothers, I'm numb when it comes to deep feelings. I don't quite know when it happened, but I might be messed up in the head, at least by therapist copay standards.

It's late and I don't feel like giving you all the whole book of my life right now, but I will give you all a little context as to how I became as emotionless as I am. This is going to be confessions on speed, so keep up.

Ready?

Last of three kids, older brother, good . . . no, great parents. Older brother hated the crap outta me (no clue why . . . well, I have some ideas), nerdy kid, jumped badly at fourteen, almost raped at gunpoint at fourteen by some random mofo (had my first nut at the same time), lost my virginity at eighteen, shot at eighteen (doctor said I'd never walk the same again ... proved him wrong), arrested for first-degree murder at twenty (though I never killed anyone), sentenced to a dozen plus five at twenty-two, released at thirty, doing great things for myself and others since then.

LOL, maybe I need some therapy. I don't know.

What I do know is that I meet great women who want to love me, who I want to love back, at least in my mind, but I have a hard time replicating that want in my heart. So, y'all are talking about loving, and I'm talking about loving. I love myself and others to the bitter end, and I'm proud of myself for surviving so much unscathed. I'm the easiest person to get along with, or disagree with.

I write well. That's what folks tell me. I speak well. That's what folks tell me. I inspire others. That's what folks tell me. Don't get me wrong, I believe all of that stuff, and I thank God for it (I was raised as a Jehovah's Witness, BTW, though I'm not really an active JW right now because I drink and screw and all that good stuff, though I don't cuss on the regular), but all this surviving and experience is so fucking much at times. You know, my pops once told me that you shouldn't suffocate the spirit, meaning you shouldn't hold in how you feel for someone.

Oh, did you expect me to give some sort of anecdotal moral to that quote, like you're taught to in English class? Like, you shouldn't leave a paragraph without finishing your point? Nah, I ain't got the answer, homies. I guess that's what I'll leave for you all to finish. You know, keep the flow going.

Bless,
Marlon Peterson

DAYDREAMING WITH D'ANDRE BROWN

"They judge us for wanting to be professional basketball players, and I get it," he tells me. "I'm trying to be great at my job. That's what I'm doing. How many of us can ever say we're working an honest job we love and chasing a dream? What's wrong with that?"

D'Andre Brown is not rich; nor is he comfortable. Most folks in Brown's hometown of Poughkeepsie, New York, don't know he averaged 22, 10, and 5 in a professional league called the Mongolian National Basketball Association. People in airports around the world see a six-foot-five frame, long tatted arms, dunking scars on his wrists, hands as expansive as spiderwebs, gear slightly less weird-boy-fresh than Russell Westbrook's, and they wonder, often aloud, if Brown is a professional athlete they should know.

"I'm a baller," he tells me, sitting outside the gym where we met ten years ago. "That's all people need to know. That's my profession."

"So what," I tell him. "The kind of balling you do, isn't that more like a part-time job? Don't you want to actually have a profession?"

"I have a profession," he smirks. "I told you. I'm a baller."

"You get insurance for balling?" I ask him. "Professions can come with insurance."

"I'm doing what makes me happy and healthy," he tells me. "And I'm getting paid for it."

Brown eats, sleeps, and travels the world off his ability to help professional teams in Mexico, Costa Rica, the Dominican Republic, and recently, Mongolia, put a twenty-two-ounce orange ball through a hole more times than the opposing team. "That," he wants to convince me, "is the only thing real ballers do. I don't need insurance for that."

"That is exactly why you need insurance. Look at Lenny Cooke and Iverson," I tell him. "They were real ballers, too, until they weren't. Don't you think all young Black men need multiple plans, or at least two dreams, nowadays?"

"Word?" he says, slowly shaking his head and looking past me. "This is where we're going with this interview, Kiese? You gonna tell me to pull my pants up and take off my hoodie next?"

I met Brown after I'd come to work at Vassar College in Poughkeepsie, from graduate school at Indiana University. Before moving north at twenty years old, I grew up in Jackson, Mississippi, a city that helped produce blue-chip ballers: James Robinson, Lindsey Hunter, Othella Harrington, Jerrod Ward, Ryan Lorthridge, Ronnie Henderson, Trey Johnson, Mo Williams, and Monta Ellis.

At some point in junior high or high school, thousands of Black boys in Jackson believed we, too, were destined for the NBA because we could shoot the 3, or touch the top of the square, or knock down a mid-range jump shot with ease. Realistically, we were Black boys whose baller dreams far eclipsed our baller talent, and Jackson was small enough that nearly all of us had some relationship with real ballers who were literally some of the best players in the country.

Most of us could point to that one day, in someone's backyard, at the Air Base, at Lake Hico, at the Y, or in a high school gymnasium, when one of those real ballers dunked, blocked, no-looked, or shot the air right out of our NBA aspirations.

For me, it was the night I came back to Jackson for Christmas break. I had made the varsity team the previous year as a ninth grader at St. Joe High School in Jackson, and spent my tenth-grade year playing junior varsity at nationally ranked DeMatha High School in Hyattsville, Maryland. During the Christmas break, I watched a sophomore I played pickup with named Othella Harrington make every shot he attempted in warm-ups, the first half, halftime, and the second half of a game at Murrah High School. Harrington finished with over 40 points, 12 dunks, and over 20 rebounds, and hardly played the fourth quarter.

The next year, Harrington and Jason Kidd were the number-one-ranked juniors in the country, and I started imagining life as a rapper, teacher, or writer.

Brown had a far different experience. Though there were plenty of supremely skilled, slightly older players in Poughkeepsie, like Renard Brown and Dasham Allah, he'd never seen a nationally ranked basketball player born and raised in Poughkeepsie.

I met Brown playing in Vassar's gym during the summer of 2003. At sixteen, he had a forty-inch vertical, the ability to finish and size that I didn't see in a lot of younger players in the area.

Brown told me the second time I played with him that he was going to the NBA. He also told me that he had never played a quarter of organized basketball because of poor grades.

Before his tenth-grade season even started, Brown and one of his best friends, Stef Singleton, went into the Arlington High School gym, where the cheerleaders left their purses, cellphones, and book bags during a football game.

81

One cheerleader's cellphone left the gym in Brown's pocket.

A couple of days later, a cop knocked on the door of his Canterbury Garden apartment. After the arrest, his high school coach said that no matter how good Brown was, he and the other assistant coaches didn't feel comfortable with a thief on the team.

"They didn't trust me," Brown tells me with a deep sigh. "It's deeper than that, but in the end, I should have known I had a shorter leash because of who I was, you know? I just messed up. Bad. No excuses."

The following summer, Brown was admitted to a school in New York City called Our Savior New American School, after one of the coaches saw him play at the Stony Brook basketball camp. Oumar Sylla, who later played at Richmond, and Juan Diego Tello Palacios, who later played at Louisville, were on the team when Brown arrived.

"Our Savior was the first place I'd ever really second-guessed my skills. Tello was the best I'd ever seen at that point. Period. And Oumar just murdered people on defense," Brown says, leaning back in his chair. "He was so good that he made you second-guess every move you wanted to make. He was the first player to show me that good defense had to be played offensively. I never forgot that."

Brown says his Our Savior team regularly competed against future NBA players like Rudy Gay, C. J. Watson, Leon Powe, Sebastian Telfair, Joey Dorsey, and Danny Green.

"I didn't respect those dudes at all," Brown tells me. "No one on my team respected them. And they didn't respect us either. Maybe it was a New York thing. We just figured, 'Hey, they gotta stand in front of us just like we gotta stand in front of them.'"

Brown came off the bench and contributed significantly his first year at Our Savior. He received a number of letters from Division I programs and claims his coaches at Our Savior told him he would move into the starting lineup the following year. Over the summer, Our Savior picked up three recruits from France and Brown was coming off the bench again. Though his first year at Our Savior had been a success on and off the court, Brown felt misled by his coaches.

"My problem was my attitude," he says. "I just didn't think anyone was really better than me, which meant that no one could coach me. I remember playing in the same tournament where LeBron's team was playing. I didn't even think LeBron was better than me. It's weird but I'm serious. If you had better numbers than me, I assumed it was because of the system you played in, or because you were more coachable than me. The thing was, I never learned to be coachable because I was never coached."

A tiny prep school called Christian Missionary & Industrial School, from my hometown, of Jackson, Mississippi, traveled to play Our Savior early in Brown's second season. Two of Brown's friends from Poughkeepsie, Tatum Butler and Ricky Bailey, were doing postgrad years at CM&I. Our Savior beat the brakes off CM&I that night, but Brown didn't play nearly as much as he wanted to. After the game, Brown talked to the CM&I coach about his situation.

An hour later, CM&I had a new player on its bus named D'Andre Brown. He was headed down to Jackson, Mississippi.

On January 2, 2004, a month after Brown left Our Savior for CM&I, a van carrying Brown's former teammates flipped on North Carolina Highway 150. One of Brown's closest friends, Kevin Mormin, a seven-foot-three junior center from Paris, was killed in the accident. Three other players ended up in critical condition.

"I made a bad decision leaving Our Savior the way I did, but that bad decision, it literally saved my life. On most of our trips, I sat right across from Kevin."

Reeling from the death of his friend, Brown tried to make the most of his experience in a new environment. "Everybody was nice in Mississippi. We stayed with the headmaster sometimes and with a host family other times. I thought Poughkeepsie had poverty, but you don't even know poverty until you see how they live in Mississippi. I don't know how y'all do it down there. I remember putting sheets of loose-leaf paper underneath our palms when we did push-ups in the house just so roaches wouldn't crawl over our hands."

Brown earned a B average during his time at CM&I. He says he had every intention of playing for Florida International after he graduated. "I passed my ACT, but I was late getting the information to the [NCAA] Clearinghouse, so the coach suggested I go to Daytona Beach Community College until all the paperwork was taken care of. Daytona held my transcript. I put myself in the worst position of looking for a hookup, and when that hookup didn't come through, I was back to square one."

After less than a semester, Brown was back in Poughkeepsie. His new plan was to take courses at Dutchess Community College and hopefully transfer to a Division I or II program after a year.

On the morning on December 5, 2005, Brown got a call that a Cadillac SUV belonging to his childhood friend Stef Singleton had been abandoned over on Corlies Avenue. When Brown got to Corlies, he saw Stef's SUV surrounded by uniformed and plainclothes policemen.

"They described the dude who was shot and that description didn't match Stef, so I figured someone must have tried to jack him and Stef just did what he had to do to defend himself."

Brown managed to get closer to the SUV and eventually saw Singleton's body slumped in the driver's seat.

"I needed to be home when Stef got murdered." Brown stands up for the first time during our conversation. "Even if

I was somewhere far away like California, I would have come back home after Stef died. I would have had to. Bad decisions led me back to Poughkeepsie, but that's where I needed to be."

Brown fell into a deep depression after Singleton's murder and didn't leave his house for four months. He stayed away from organized basketball for the next three years. "That was the only time in my life that I can say I gave up on my dream. It's more like I gave up on dreaming altogether. I think I'd always used basketball to like, cope, to bring some joy to my life. After Stef got murdered, I don't know man. It's just, Stef was a dreamer, too. Just like me."

In 2008, Brown was recruited by Indian River Junior College, in Fort Pierce, Florida. Brown ended up averaging close to 8 points and 4 rebounds his first season, and upped those averages to 11 and 6 his second season. Then, he says, "the school went from a two-year junior college to a four-year state school."

While Brown was preparing for his junior year in 2010–11, at what is now called Indian River State College, he got a call from an agent saying that a league in Mexico wanted him to come play professionally.

"I didn't care about NCAA eligibility," he says. "I thought playing professional basketball, even if it was in Mexico, would get me closer to the NBA than playing two more years at Indian River. I couldn't wait for tomorrow."

At this point in the conversation, Brown is watching me shake my head. He wants to talk about the past three years of his life he's spent playing professional basketball in Mexico, Costa Rica, the Dominican Republic, and recently Mongolia. "Go ahead and say it," he says.

"You already know what I think," I tell him. "I just know you'd have more stability and more choices in your life if you'd stayed in school and earned that degree."

"It's good to be getting paid to do what I love," he finally says. "But my dream is the NBA. I'm closer to the NBA than I was when we met. Plus, I'm working. I have a job. You see how many of us are unemployed out here?"

"But you already reached a dream," I tell him. "At some point, we all wanted to get paid to play. You don't get it, but you already reached the dream we all had. You traveled the world off of basketball. Who can say that? Don't you think it's time to start working a real job?"

"A lot of people who come from places like us, they chase that fast money because tomorrow, you could be locked up," he tells me. "Or worse. They always say that we should be working, but they never look at it from our perspective. That's what LeBron meant when he said, 'I'm not even supposed to be here.' People think he meant on that stage, but for so many of us, it means just being alive doing what we love. We aren't supposed to be here. You aren't supposed to be here writing and teaching." Brown's left hand is loosely balled up in a huge fist. "But you are here. And I'm proud of you. Be proud of me. I understand the system, Kiese. I ain't chasing fast money. I ain't even chasing slow money, either. I worked for almost nothing in Mexico. In the Dominican Republic, they tried to jerk me out of my whole check. But still, I was working a job I loved, chasing a dream. And I'm better at my profession today than I was a few months ago. I'm a good basketball player, and I'm still getting better."

Karl Egner, an older guy who manages the gym, tells us it's time to leave. Brown grabs his ball and his bag. I grab my computer and my notebook. Out in the parking lot, I ask if he needs a ride to his mother's house.

"I know that people think I should be chasing a regular job right now," he tells me from the passenger seat of my car. "I'm not dumb. Right now, I'm working. And my work took me to countries I never even knew existed."

I'm quiet for a few seconds before laughing while admitting that I just got a passport a few months ago in order to go to an American Studies conference in Puerto Rico.

"But you don't need a passport for Puerto Rico," he tells me and laughs for about three blocks. "You're a professor at Vassar College and you didn't even know that Puerto Rico is a U.S. territory?"

I'm laughing with him.

"You see what I'm saying then?" he says. "People like us, we don't get to go to Mongolia following our dreams. Look at you. You got a good job, a nice car, books, and you just got a passport. You're like a role model to us, but you ain't even been out of the country. That's crazy, nigga."

We reach the driveway of his mother's house.

"Good look on the ride," he tells me. "You think they'll publish this even though I'm not in the NBA yet?"

"Maybe they will," I tell him. "The story is all about the politics of American dreaming, not just the NBA, right?"

"If you say so," he says, with one foot out of the car.

I ask him one more time to at least think about life after basketball if he doesn't make the NBA. I don't tell him that before our conversation I asked my college coach, Satch Sullinger, what advice I should give D'Andre.

"You play the game the way you live your life," Coach Sullinger told me. "Bad players fight their roles. Good players accept their roles. Great players dominate their roles. D'Andre has to decide who he is going to be on and off the court. You can't solve a problem using the same line of thinking that created the problem. Hurt me with the truth but never comfort me with a lie."

I take Coach's advice to heart and decide not to let Brown leave my car without telling him my truth. Without looking at him, I tell him that I want to him consider full-time teaching, coaching, or the creation of a mentoring program. I tell him that 50 percent of the first ten NBA draft picks are out of the league after two years, and twelve of the first twenty selected are generally gone after two. I tell him that by age twenty-eight, even if he made the league, he would be two years from being considered an older NBA veteran. Finally, I tell him that it's not fair that so many folks in the nation obsessively rely on a tough love approach for young Black men chasing athletic dreams, yet have nothing to say about broke aspiring writers, photographers, soccer players, filmmakers, and small business owners. "But," I tell him while finally looking at him, "I think fear is stopping you from accepting the possibility of multiple dreams. I think you're afraid to change and dream more than one dream."

"I can't lie to you," he finally says, both feet out of the car. "I just can't see giving up on my dream, or my job, just because it's not somebody else's dream of what happiness is." He reaches his huge right hand through the window and gives me some dap. "I'm working, Kiese, and I'm happy. I'm getting better at my job, and I'm working every day. How many people like us can say that they're working and they're happy? I'm not stupid. I know the NBA ain't right around the corner. But I'm working. I'm happier doing this work than any other work in the world. Right now, I know it's not what you or anyone else reading this will want to hear, but I'm working. I'm happy. That's enough for me."

I think, but don't tell D'Andre Brown, that I am working too, though I am not happy. I think, but don't tell D'Andre Brown, that deep unhappiness, and really this sprawling spiritual emptiness, is, shamefully, enough for me. I think, but don't tell D'Andre Brown, that his dreaming inspires me to find my way back to Mississippi, the place I do my most courageous dreaming. And witnessing.

YOU ARE THE
SECOND PERSON

You know that any resemblance to real places, spaces, people, time, or things is purely coincidental.

Alone, you sit on the floor of your apartment thinking about evil, honesty, that malignant growth in your hip, your dead uncle, letters you should have written, the second person, and stretch marks. You're wearing an XXL T-shirt you plan on wearing the day your novel comes out. The front of the T-shirt says, "What's a real Black writer?" The back reads, "Fuck you. Pay me." You open your computer. With a scary pain in your hip, you inhale and force a crooked smile before reading an email from Brandon Farley, your fifty-four-year-old Black editor.

"The success of your book will be partially dependent on readers who have a different sensibility than your intended audience," he writes. "As I've already said to you, too many sections of the book feel forced for the purpose of discussing racial politics. Think social media. Think comment sections. Those white people buy books, too, bro. Readers, especially white readers, are tired of Black writers playing the wrong race card. If you're gonna play it (and I think you should) play it right. Look at Tarantino. He is about to fool all these people into believing they are watching a Black movie with *Django*. I guarantee you that whiteness will anchor almost every scene. That's one model you should think about.

"Also, Black men don't read. And if they did, they wouldn't read this kind of fiction. So you might think of targeting bougie Black women readers. Bougie Black women love plot. They love romance with predictable Boris Kodjoe–type characters. Or they love strong sisters caught up in professional hijinks who have no relationships with other sisters. Think about what holds a narrative like *Scandal* together. Real Black writers make the racial, class, gender, and sexual politics of their work implicit. Very implicit. The age of the 'race narrative' is over, bro. As is, the only way your book would move units is if Oprah picked it for her book club. That's not happening. Oprah only deals with real Black writers."

You begin typing, "Hey Brandon, this is my fourteenth thorough revision for you in four years. I know I'm not changing your mind and that's fine. Thanks for telling me what real Black writers do and what Oprah likes. You never told me you met her. Anyway, the Black teenagers in my book are actually purposefully discussing 'racial politics' in awkwardly American ways. Their race and racial politics, like their sexuality and sexual politics, is somehow tied to every part of their character. My book is unapologetically an American race novel, among other things. I'm still not sure why you bought the book if you didn't dig the vision."

You push send on the email before opening up the word.doc you just defended. You jump to chapter nine. Thirty minutes later, a section of the book where an older queer coach tries to impart a strange "them/us" racial understanding to your narrator is cut because it "explicitly discusses racial politics."

You call your editor names that hurt, muddied misanthropic names you pride yourself on never calling any human being, while looking out the tall window of your second-floor apartment in Poughkeepsie, New York.

A barefoot white boy with a red-and-black lumberjack shirt

is outside sitting under an oak tree. He's doing that walkie-talkie thing on his phone that you fucking hate. You can tell he's telling the truth and lying at the same time.

"*You fucking* hurt me more than anyone in my whole life," he says. "I couldn't hate *you* . . . I just don't trust *you* . . . *You*'re the second person who has done this to me. *You*'re the one who said you tell the truth . . . *You* started this." The white boy is scratching his sack with the thumb of his left hand and using his big toe to make designs in the dirt in front of him. "*You* ruined my life and hurt me way more than I hurt *you*. It's always all about *you*."

You wonder about the second person on the end of the phone. Is the second person a woman or man? Is s/he listening to the lumberjack on speakerphone? Is s/he wishing the lumberjack would hurry up and finish so s/he can run and get a two-for-one special on Peanut Buster Parfaits from Dairy Queen? You know far too well why a first or third person could self-righteously claim innocence in matters of love and loss, but you can't figure out why the lumberjack is scratching his sack with his thumb and making dirt rainbows with his big toe.

Looking down at the browning "s" key on your keyboard, you think more hateful thoughts about your editor, your ex-girlfriend, skinny people, and fat young Black men. These thoughts distract you from the pain in your hip, the dirt on your hands.

For five years, Brandon Farley, your editor, has had you waiting.

You remember the acidic sweetness in Grandmama's voice when you told her you'd just signed a two-book deal with "KenteKloth Books," the most popular African-American imprint in the country. New York fall felt like Mississippi winter as Grandmama came out of her second diabetic coma.

"We are so proud of you, baby," Grandmama whispered

over the phone from Forest, Mississippi. "Just remember that God gave you five senses and whatever health you got for a reason. When they gone, they gone, but if you don't use them best you can while you got them, ain't a bigger fool in the world than that fool in the mirror."

Six months before your first novel's initial scheduled publication date of June 2009, you stopped hearing from Brandon Farley. He didn't answer your calls or respond to emails. You gave up and called the publisher of KenteKloth in February.

"Oh, Brandon didn't tell you?" his boss asked. "He's no longer with us, but your book has been picked up by Nathalie Bailey. She'll call you in a few days."

Your lungs whistled, crashed, and slipped into the heels of your feet. You told yourself it would be okay. Then you trudged your sexy ass to the International House of Pancakes.

Three hours later, you were full, fatter than you wanted to be, less sexy than you were, and you had found a way to reach Brandon Farley at home. Brandon apologized for not telling you that he wasn't seeing eye-to-eye with his boss. He promised you that Nathalie Bailey was a friend of his who would do right by both of your novels.

A week later, you got a call from Nathalie. "It's a hard sell for Black literary fiction these days," she told you. "But I like what you're doing. You're on your way to becoming a real Black writer. It's a gorgeous book with big messy ideas and we've got to work hard and fast. But I'd love for you to let me take this book to publication. It's a winner."

You felt a comfort with Nathalie, but you didn't want to be as impulsive as you had been with Brandon. "Can I have a few days to think about it?" you asked her. "Just to make sure."

A few days passed and you planned on calling Nathalie at 4:00 p.m. on a Thursday. At 3:00 p.m., you got a call from a 212 number. Before you had a book deal, 917 and 212 numbers were like slimming mirrors; they made you think, *Damn nigga, you ain't that disgusting at all.*

On the other end of 917 and 212 numbers were agents, editors, or an ex telling you she was sorry and she missed sharing a heartbeat.

"Hello," you answered, trying to sound busy and country at the same time.

"Hi."

It was Brandon Farley.

After a few minutes of spin where Brandon Farley showed you how much he remembered about your book and how happy he was to be the new senior editor of young adult fiction at the widely acclaimed "Duck Duck Goose Publishing Company," he said, "... all that to say, we really want your book."

"Word?"

"Word up, bro!" Brandon laughed. It was the first time any Black man on earth had ever called you "bro" with a long "o."

"Bro," he said it again, "I will pay you more for one book than you got for two over at KenteKloth. I'll want an option of first refusal on the second. But that'll still give you the kind of flexibility you want."

"Are you serious?" you asked. "Only thing is I'm a little worried about changing the subtext and the darkness and the metafictive stuff if it's gonna be marketed as a young adult book. The ending ain't really pretty."

"You'd be surprised at the possibilities in young adult fiction," he told you. "Listen, bro, young adults will read it. This is adult literary fiction with mass appeal. You won't have to make many changes at all and we can get you a pub date of June 2010."

"But what about Nathalie?" you asked.

"Bro, you're the second person to ask me about her." He

scoffed, sounding like a hungry hip-hop mogul. You hated even imagining using the word "scoffed."

"It's business, bro. Never personal. You'll have to get out of that contract over there. And I've got the perfect agent for you. She's this wonderful fine sister over at Chatham Ward & Associates named Bobbie Winslow. Look her up. Bobbie'll take care of everything if you decide to go with us."

You smiled and forgave him for four or five "bros" too many.

Later that night, Bobbie, the perfect agent/fine sister, called from a 212 number and asked you to send her the other pieces you were working on. By 8:00 p.m., you'd sent her the book Brandon wanted, another novel, and a rough draft of some essays you'd been working on. By 3:00 a.m., she emailed you and said, "We want you. You're the second person I've said this to in five years, but I think you could change the trajectory of African-American contemporary literature. You've got the makings of what Brandon calls 'a real Black writer.' I'm so excited about the new projects you're working on. If you sign with Chatham Ward, we'll have our lawyers get you out of the deal with Nathalie in the next week or so and Brandon says he can get us half the advance in three weeks. I'll be in touch."

You never contacted Nathalie, but a few days later, Bobbie, the perfect agent/fine sister did. "Nathalie is so fucking pissed," she said a few days later, "but all's fair in love, war, and business." As you wondered whether this was love, war, or business, you and your perfect agent/fine sister waited and waited and waited for Brandon to deliver.

Six months later, three months after your initial publication date of June 2009, Brandon offered you substantially less money than he had promised and a publication date a year later than the one he'd verbally agreed to.

"Pardon me for saying this," your perfect agent said over

the phone from a different 212 number, "but Brandon Farley is a bona fide b— ass nigga for fucking us out of thousands of dollars and pushing the pub date back to June 2011. He's just not professional. I'm wondering if this was just some ploy to get you away from KenteKloth. He's been trying to take all his authors away from them as a way of fucking the company."

"I don't get it," you said, shamefully excited that your agent had used "fuck," "b— ass," and "nigga" in one conversation.

"So Brandon acquired this wonderful list of new literary Black authors at KenteKloth, and they were all going to work with Nathalie after he was basically fired from the company. Nathalie and the house were going to get credit for a lot of his work. Do you get it now? We got caught up in something really nasty."

You finally got your first edit letter from Brandon Farley the following July. In addition to telling you that the tone of the piece was far too dark and that you needed an obvious redemptive ending, Brandon wrote, "There's way too much racial politics in this piece, bro. You're writing to a multicultural society, but you're not writing multiculturally."

You wondered out loud what writing "multiculturally" actually meant and what kind of Black man would write the word "bro" in an email.

"Bro, we need this book to come down from 284 pages to 150," he said. "We're going to have to push the pub date back again, too. I'm thinking June 2012. Remember," he wrote, "it's business. I think you should start from scratch but keep the spirit. Does the narrator really need to be a Black boy? Does the story really need to take place in Mississippi? The Percy Jackson demographic," he wrote. "That's a big part of the audience for your novel. Read it over the weekend. Real Black writers adjust to the market, bro, at least for their first novels."

By the time you found out Percy Jackson wasn't the name

of a conflicted Black boy from Birmingham, but a fake-ass Harry Potter who saved the gods of Mount Olympus, you were already broken. Meanwhile, someone you claimed to love told you that you were letting your publishing failure turn you into a monster. She said that you were becoming the kind of human being you had always despised. You defended yourself against the truth and, really, against responsibility, as American monsters and American murderers tend to do, and you tried to make this person feel as absolutely worthless, confused, and malignant as you felt. Later that night, you couldn't sleep, and instead of diving back into the fiction, for the first time in your life, you wrote the sentence, "I've been slowly killing myself and others close to me, just like my uncle."

Something else was wrong, too. Your body no longer felt like your body, and you doubted whether your Grandmama would ever see your work before one of you died.

Two years after the original scheduled publication date for your first book, there was still no book. Questions fell like dominoes. *Why would Brandon buy the book?* you kept asking yourself. *Why would that fucker get you out of a contract for a book he didn't want?* your perfect agent kept asking you. *Why'd you promise stuff you couldn't deliver?* you asked Brandon on the phone.

"The book doesn't just have Duck Duck Goose's name on it," you told him, slightly aware of what happens when keeping it real goes wrong. "My name is on that shit, too. That means, on some level, it ain't business. I feel like you want me to lie. I read and write for a living, Brandon. I see the shit that's out there. I've read your other books. I see your goofy book covers looking like greasy children's menus at Applebee's. I ain't putting my name on a fucking greasy Applebee's menu. I'm not. Don't front like it's about quality. You, and maybe your editorial board, don't think you can sell this book because you don't believe Black Southern audiences read literary shit. And that's fine. Maybe you're right. If you didn't believe in it, why buy it in the first place? Look, I can create an audience for this novel with these essays I've been writing," you tell him. "It sounds stupid, but I can. I just need to know that you're committed to really publishing this book. Do you believe in the vision or not?"

After a long pause during which you could hear Brandon telling his assistant, Jacques, to leave the room and get him a warm bear claw with extra glaze, he said, "Bro, you're the second person to complain to me this morning about how I do my job. The first person had a bit more tact. Honestly," he said, "reading your work has been painful. It's business. Take that folksy shit back to Mississippi. I did you a favor. Don't forget that. You're just not a good writer, bro. Goodbye."

The next morning you got an email from Brandon with the following message,

"Hey Wanda, I finished the revision this afternoon. It totally kicks ass. Congrats. I've sent back a few line edits, but it's brilliant. Move over Teju and Chimamanda. There's a new African writer on the scene showing these Black American writers how it's done. I'm so proud of you. Always darkest before the dawn, Wanda. It feels so empowering to work with the future of contemporary diasporic literature. Tell David hi for me. Best, Brandon."

Your name was not and never will be "Wanda."

You opened up Facebook to the News Feed page and found that Brandon, your Facebook friend, had posted the covers of recently published and forthcoming books he'd edited. Wanda's book, and all the other covers, really did look like greasy children's menus at Applebee's. Your eyes watered as you googled the published authors Brandon had signed two years after he signed you. You wanted your name on an Applebee's menu, too.

Even though you were fatter than you'd ever been and the

joints in your hip got rustier and more decayed every day, parts of you were a rider. Yeah, Brandon bombed first, you thought, but right there, you felt determined to get your novel out by any means necessary so you could thank him in the acknowledgments:

". . . And a special thanks to that shape-shifting cowardly ol' lying ass, Brandon Farley, the untrustworthy editing-cause-he-can't-write-a-lick-ass Tom who'd sell out his mama for a gotdamn glazed bear claw as long as the bear claw had been half-eaten by a white librarian named Jacques or Percy Jackson. I know where you live. And I got goons. Can you see me now? Goooood. Congrats, BRO."

Instead you wrote, "Not sure why you sent that email intended for Wanda, Brandon. I hope we both appreciate the distinction between what's marketable and what's possible. Glad you're having success with some of your authors. I think you should give my books a chance to breathe, too. Thanks for the inspiration. Tell Wanda congratulations."

Brandon never responded to your email.

You stayed in your bedroom for weeks writing essays to your dead uncle, your Grandmama, the son and daughter you didn't have. Outside of that bedroom, and outside of your writing life, you'd fully become a liar *unafraid* to say I love you, *too willing* to say I'm sorry, *unwilling* to change the ingredients of your life, which meant that you'd gobbled up your own heart and you were halfway done gobbling up the heart of a woman who loved you.

One Tuesday near the end of spring, you couldn't move your left leg or feel your toes, and you'd been sweating through your mattress for a month. You knew there was something terribly wrong long before your furry-fingered doctor, with tiny hands and eyebrows to die for, used the words "malignant growth."

"It won't be easy," the doctor told you the Friday before

Spring Break. "You're the second person I've diagnosed with this today, but there's still a chance we can get it without surgery. You said you've been living with the pain for three years? Frankly, I'm worried about you," the doctor said. "You seem like you're holding something in. Fear is okay, you know? Do you have any questions?"

You watched the doctor's eyebrows sway like black wheat. They looked like a hyper four-year-old had gone buckwild with a fistful of black crayons. "I like your eyebrows," you told the doctor. "I don't know what's wrong with me. I just want my Grandmama to think I'm a real writer."

"I'd actually like to recommend therapy in addition to the treatment," the doctor told you before he walked you out the door.

For the next few months, you took the treatment he gave you and prided yourself on skipping the therapy. You told no one about the malignant growth in your hip, not even the person whose heart you were eating. Though you could no longer run or trust, you could eat and you could hate. So you ate, and you ate, and you hated, until, sixty-eight pounds and five months later, you were finally unrecognizable to yourself.

One Sunday near the end of spring, after talking to your two family members who were both killing themselves slowly, too, you made the decision to finally show the world the blues you'd been creating. You also decided to finish revising the novel without Brandon.

"The whole time I'd been in those woods," you wrote in one of the last scenes in the book, "I'd never stopped and looked up."

You spent the next four months of your life skipping treatments for your hip and getting a new draft of the novel done. You didn't dumb down the story for Brandon, for multiculturalism, or for school boards you'd never see. You wrote an honest book to Paul Beatty, Margaret Walker Alexander, Cassandra Wilson, Big K.R.I.T., Octavia Butler, Gangsta Boo, your little cousins, and all your teachers.

You prayed on it and sent the book to Brandon in July. You told him that you had created a post-Katrina, Afrofuturist, time-travel-ish, Black Southern love story filled with adventure, metafiction, and mystery. You wanted to call the book *Long Division* after one of the characters' insistence on showing work in the past, present, and future.

"It's a book I'm proud of," you wrote in the letter attached to the manuscript. "It's something I needed to read when I was a teenager in Mississippi. Shit, it's something I need to read now. I'm willing to work on it. Just let me know if you get the vision."

Brandon responded the same day that he would check it out over the weekend and get back to you with his thoughts.

Four months later, he finally sent an email: "Ultimately, the same problems exist in this draft that were in the other drafts." Brandon ended the email, "We need more traditional adventure. We need to know less about the relationships between the characters, less racial politics, and more about the adventure. You need to explain how the science fiction works, bro. No one is going to believe Black kids from Mississippi traveling through time talking about institutional racism. It's way too meandering. Kill the metafictive angle. You haven't earned the right to pull that off. This is still painful. I'm convinced you really do not want to be a real Black writer, bro. The success of your book will be partially dependent on readers who have a different sensibility than your intended audience..."

Still too ashamed to really reckon with your disease or your failures, and too cowardly to own your decisions, you stretched your legs out on the floor of your living room and cried your eyes out. After crying, laughing, and wondering if love really could save all the people public policy forgot, you grabbed a pad and scribbled, "Alone, you sit on the floor..."

After writing for about two hours, you wondered why you'd started the piece with "Alone, you . . ." You are the "I" to no one in the world, not even yourself.

You've eviscerated people who loved you when they made you the second person in their lives, when they put the relationship's needs ahead of your wants. And you've been eviscerated for the same thing.

You're not a monster. You're not innocent.

You look down at the browning "s" key on your keyboard. You don't know how long you'll live. No one does. You don't know how long you'll have two legs. You know that it's time to stop letting your anger and hate toward Brandon Farley and your publishing failure be more important than the art of being human and healthy. You know it's time to admit to yourself, your writing, and folks who love you that you're at least the second person to feel like you're really good at slowly killing yourself and others in America.

"Sorry your reads have been so painful, Brandon," you start typing. "I want to get healthy. That means not only that I need to be honest, but also that I've got to take my life back and move to a place where I no longer blame you for failure. I've thought and said some terrible things about you. I've blamed you for the breaking of my body and the breaking of my heart. I really believed that you and your approval would determine whether I was a real Black writer, worthy of real self-respect and real dignity.

"There was something in my work, something in me that resonated with your work and something in you. We are connected. I'm not sure what happens next. No young writer, real or not, leaves an iconic press before their first book comes, right? Whatever. I can't put my name on the book that you want written and it's apparent that you won't put your company's name on the book I want read. We tried, Brandon, but life is long and short. I've written my way out of death and destruction before. I'm trying to do it again. I think I'm done with the New York publishing thing for a while. I'm through with the editors, the agents, and all that stress. No hate at all. It's just not for me. I can't be healthy dealing with all of that. I've been cooking up a lot of stuff. Most of it is bad. Some of it is legendary. I'll get my work out to my folks and if they want more, I'll show them. If not, that's fine. I'm a writer. I write.

"I'm sorry and sorrier that sorry is rarely enough. God gave me senses and a little bit of health. It's time for me to use them the best that I can. Thanks for the shot. Good luck. I hope you like the work I'm doing. Not sure if you'll vibe with it, but I know it's black, blue, Mississippi, new, and honest. I'm a not a bro, Brandon. You ain't either. Thanks again for everything."

You look up.

You close your eyes.

You breathe.

You look down and you keep on writing, revising, and imagining, because that's what real Black writers do.

HIP-HOP STOLE MY SOUTHERN BLACK BOY

In 1998, I stood in the basement bathroom of Mudd Library at Oberlin College and asked myself, *Quick, Kie, what in the hell is a cipher?* It was a question I couldn't ask out loud, as I was speaking of the word, not *Tha Cypher*, a magazine that Rich Santiago, from the Bronx, and David Jacobs were creating outside the bathroom. The word "cipher," I remembered had initially crept up on me in a much smaller Central Mississippi bathroom back in 1992.

Back then, fifteen minutes into our lunch period, seven of us descended into what we called the B-Boy bathroom. B-Boy for us meant neither Breaker Boy, Bad Boy, nor Bronx Boy; it meant Black Boy. There, B. Dazzle, who was the little brother of god-emcee Kamikaze of the group Crooked Lettaz, chaired a lyrical demolition of Stacy "King Slender" Hill.

I slouched between two urinals, hands cupped over mouth, providing a weak beat box while B. Dazzle went on and on and on . . . Every Black Boy in the bathroom caught a vibe from his lyrics, or at least we acted like we did, *in spite* of the fact that we were the Southern Niggas who needed to get wiser, and *because* we were the Southern Niggas who ironically felt wiser and more real just by listening to B. Dazzle. The seven of us, including the just-dissed King Slender, bobbed our heads and pumped our fists like we knew what everything in his rhyme, including his "cipher," really meant.

You had to be a B-Boy to enter our space. No Black girls, Asians, or white folks stepped foot in the B-Boy bathroom when we rocked it. In my imagination, I always see K. Parry, a gregarious, theatrical, give-peace-a-chance white guy trying to Rocky his way into our space with some sharp wit and dramatic vocal bombast. This large thespian wobbles into the bathroom in some stone-washed cutoffs and penny loafers. He proceeds to spit a monologue that doesn't even rhyme before getting sliced up by the previously demolished King Slender, who says something like, ". . . I'm Clubber Lang, K. Parry, not Stacy the Hill / This the Nigga version of Rocky and Balboa gettin' killed." King Slender ends it by saying, "Live on, Apollo Creed."

Classic.

Black girls couldn't be a real part of our space because they were busy with their own rituals. Plus, getting caught in the opposite sex's bathroom got you suspended for a week. We cracked open the door of the bathroom just enough so the Black girls could hear. And what they heard, probably more than our actual rhymes, was our responses to our rhymes. As the beatbox-accompanied boasts, confessionals, and critiques moved from between urinals and stalls out the door of the bathroom into the hallway, the Black girls, white folks, Asians, and wack niggas could only consume and interrogate the sound, not the creative culture or experience from whence that sound sprang. Our cipher was off-limits to them, B. Dazzle told me. And quiet as it was kept, we wanted it that way. We wanted the Black girls, especially, to need to hear what we were up to from a distance, but we refused to conceive them as our primary audience. Conversely, they kept us out of their private rituals, too.

From our position, the Black girls in the hall were positioned in the same way we were positioned as Southern eavesdroppers of New York hip-hop. Some would get close as they could to the crack of the door, but they could never come all the way in. We understood that the seven Southern Black Boys in that space were private, mysterious, and desired by folk who didn't really know how or why we did what we did. That belief made us feel more powerful, possessed, closer to real hip-hop, and strangely closer to New York.

Within that B-Boy room, all of us knew that hip-hop credibility had little to do with the quality of your boast, the intensity of your critique, or the passion of your confessional. Really, it was all rooted in your hip-hop aesthetic. And that aesthetic seemed to be rooted in geography. Hip-hop and New York became unspoken adjectives in small Southern spaces like this, and one's worth in the B-Boy room was based almost solely on how hip-hop or New York the other six listeners thought you and your style were.

I had a decent bit of hip-hop credibility due to spending summers in upstate New York visiting my father (to most Black Mississippians, New York State meant New York City), but my rhyme style was too deliberate, dirty, local, filled with too many "or" words that were pronounced with a long "o" to be considered authentic New York. "Now I need no mic," I would rap, "just a slow-ass tempo / step to me wrong and mother-fucker, you in fo' / a beat down that'll go down in your history books / come try and fuck with Kie, get yo ego took." That was the favorite of my four lyrical styles. And the other three styles, though dope in their own way, sounded remarkably close to that one. In the B-Boy bathroom, my rhymes swayed the crowd, but the movement started and stopped in between those two Central Mississippi urinals. B. Dazzle, on the other hand, moved the crowd to different states, figuratively and literally, and his character was as desired and enigmatic as his rhymes.

I believed the myth was that B. Dazzle and his older brother, Kamikaze, spent summers not in Poughkeepsie, Rochester, Albany, or Syracuse, but at some cousin's place in the South

Bronx. The myth allowed me to slavishly follow when B. Dazzle chided us to use the term "hip-hop" instead of "rap," and "cipher" instead of "rap circle." "Hip-hop is more lyrical, more New York, nigga," he told me. He said it was universal, real, filled with brothers in ciphers dropping knowledge, breaking, deejaying, graffiti writing, showing, and proving, while rap music, on the ashy Black-hand side, was artistically inferior, country-sounding, and local.

Henry James didn't have to tell us that geography was fate. Shit, we knew that. The seven of us had similar dreams of being divine emcees, too, though we knew geography wouldn't allow it. Plus, our mamas and grandparents had other plans, and they made sure we became multiple dreamers who actualized boring dreams like becoming managers, counterfeiters, computer engineers, racketeers, sergeants, pimps, and college professors.

As much as parts of us tried not to be, we were country Black Boys with little to no experience with real New York hip-hop except *Yo! MTV Raps* and *Rap City*, or when the Fresh Fest came to the Coliseum or KRS-ONE came to Jackson State University. And by Mississippi standards, the seven of us weren't even that country because we were from the city of Jackson. In Jackson, and other parts of the Black Belt, we were no longer the dutiful disciples of the Holy Trinity of MCs—Kane, KRS, and Rakim. We respected the gods, but we were done exclusively eavesdropping on the rhymes coming out of New York City. West Coast music, as varied as it was, met us where we were, and truth be told, it was music we could see and hear. We also accepted that the West Coast and the Black Belt were family, and had been since the second great migration of the 1940s ushered thousands of Southern Black families to Los Angeles for jobs in the automotive and defense industries.

It's true that the South, dismissed as culturally slow, meaningless, and less hip (hop) than New York, had yet to, as Albert

Murray wrote, lyrically stylize our Southern worlds into significance. But if outsiders really listened to the musty movement behind the Geto Boyz, UGK, Eight Ball, and MJG, they would have heard the din of deeply Southern Black Boys and girls eager to keep it real *local*. We wanted to use hip-hop's brash boast, confessional, and critique to unapologetically order the chaos of our country lives through country lenses, with little regard for whether it sounded like *real* hip-hop.

We were on our way to realizing that we were blues people, familiar in some way or another with dirt. There were no skyscrapers and orange-brown projects stopping us from looking up and out. We didn't know what it was like to move in hordes, with enclosed subway trains slithering beneath our feet.

And we liked it that way.

En route to lyrical acceptance of our dirty, we met Scarface, JT Money, Ice Cube, Bun B, MC Ren, and D.O.C. And after a while, we realized that they were our cousins, our uncles, our best friends, us. We rode through Compton, Oakland, Port Arthur, and Houston the same way we rode through Jackson, Meridian, Little Rock, New Orleans, and Birmingham. We rode in long cars with windows down, bass quaking, and air fresheners sparkling like Christmas tree ornaments.

We felt pride in knowing that the greatest producer alive was an uncle from Compton and the most anticipated emcee in the history of hip-hop was a lanky brother from Long Beach. We knew, no matter what anyone in New York said, that the baddest emcee on Earth, song for song, album for album, was an aging cousin from South Central Los Angeles whose government name was O'Shea.

But B. Dazzle, through his lyrics, clothes, sensibility, and utterances of "ciphers," still reveled in being New York hip-hop. And being New York hip-hop trumped being a Southern Black Boy who wondered if New York hip-hop loved him in the early 1990s. Chicago rapper Common Sense rapped in 1994 about faithfully loving HER, a version (or virgin) of pure hip-hop who moved away from New York essence and lost her soul. We could and couldn't relate, because while the last thing on earth we admitted to wanting to be was a woman or a gay man, our love interest, nonetheless was a HE, a him. And though HE was changing, HE was still sadly New York hip-hop. Around our way, his holy local apostle was a gap-toothed brother with skills and chappy lips named B. Dazzle. The booming acoustics of the B-Boy bathroom and the B-Boy imagination were his Mecca, and since this was before the advent of player-hation, I couldn't hate. All I could do was not let on that I was starting to love a kind of hip-hop that loved me back, and try hard as hell to be down.

That was then.

Rewind (or fast-forward) back to my standing in an Oberlin College bathroom in early 1998. While Rich Santiago and D. Jakes were in the A-level of the library trying to find titles for their new hip-hop magazine, Rich had looked at me and said, "Yo Kie, what about *Tha Cypher*?" And I was on some, "Yeah man. That's it." Now, exactly why I thought *Tha Cypher* was it is where the story gets a bit shameful. At the time, when I heard "cipher," I didn't think of a tight circle of brothers taking turns boasting, critiquing, and confessing themselves into the world over a beatbox. The word "cipher" reminded me solely of B. Dazzle and my faulty obsession. It sounded industrial, sleek, masculine, New York—like if the magazine could speak, through gapped fronts, he would say, "I *am* hip-hop, son. Yah mean? What!"

And I guessed that's what Rich and them wanted in a magazine. But honestly, I understood a few hours later that I might have been too country, too dirty, too much of a Black Boy—might have smelled too many boiling chitlins, said "finna" too many times, got my ass waxed by too many switches off the chinaberry tree, comfortably ridden in too many pineconed cabs of pickup trucks—to thoroughly understand what a cipher was in 1992 or 1998. When I said "cipher" over and over again in that bathroom, with all its jaggedly dangling connotations, it sounded fake, forced, clean. *Was our Black Boy Central Mississippi space just another cipher?* The more I said the word, the more I felt like Puffy's verse in "It's All About the Benjamins," Michael Jackson's chin, Vanilla Ice's fade, Hype's *Belly*, and *Soul Train* post–Don Cornelius. I felt like a something, not a somebody, with forced style and suspect substance, a something that would go to all lengths to never acknowledge its dirtiness, a something that created pleasure in aesthetically being the opposite of a Mississippi Black Boy.

In college, like lots of Southern Black Boys, I could bring the ever fake and flexible "Word," "Nam sayin'?" or "Yo, son" where need be. But stripped of the verbal signifiers of hip-hop, I was left kinda naked. I became what I was running from in that Mississippi B-Boy bathroom in 1992, the opposite of an NYC B-Boy. I was an unrefined, red-eyed, dirty, Mississippi Black Boy looking for both acceptance and something to resist anywhere I could find it. In 1992, it was B. Dazzle and in 1998, at Oberlin, it was *Tha Cypher*. Both times, the "it" I really wanted to accept, resist, and love was New York hip-hop. But to love and resist New York hip-hop, I had to believe hip-hop and New York were ends in themselves that had little to do with Black Southern me.

And this is where it gets tricky, because by 1998 the South completely accepted its dirtiness. When Goodie Mob asked the question on its classic *Soul Food*, "What you niggas know about the Dirty South?" New York hip-hop's honest answer should have been "Yo, not a gotdamn thing, son. And we ain't really trying to know that country shit, either."

1998 was the year that the Calio Projects of New Orleans

met hip-hop. Everything Master P and No Limit put out went gold and platinum. All over the country, people claimed to be "Bout It." UGK, underground Southern glory at its rawest, was about to show Jay Z and the country how to Big Pimp. Out-kast was a few years removed from driving a Southernplay-eristic Cadillac from Atlanta to space and back with *ATLiens*, and they were about to redefine sonic chemistry with *Aque-mini*. Far from crunk, but also far from the clean bounce of Kriss Kross, Goodie Mob released a follow-up to the critically acclaimed *Soul Food* that pronounced they were *Still Standing*.

Inside the library, D. Jakes and Rich were busy trying to cre-ate a magazine that mimicked New York hip-hop ciphers, but in the town of Oberlin, Ohio, and nearby cities like Cleveland, Detroit, and St. Louis, folks were listening to and loving how Southern Black Boys were redefining hip-hop. Folks in these other cities watched these Southern artists learn what artists west of the Deep South had learned ten years earlier and Mid-west artists like Bone learned four years earlier: they under-stood that imitating and interrogating New York hip-hop was fruitless without applying that imitation and interrogation to one's local culture, one's place. This understanding was at the core of the success of N.W.A., Bone, and eventually OutKast. As great a moment as this was for the South, was there anyone who thought that Southern hip-hop would move beyond the heights it reached in 1998? How could it?

That was then.

Rewind or fast-forward to 2013. I'm standing in the bath-room of Vassar College, a college sixty-five miles north of New York City. During the last five years, I sold two blues- and hip-hop-inspired books, though they've yet to be published, and taught four different courses with hip-hop at their cen-ter, including one called "Shawn Carter: Autobiography of an Autobiographer." Many of my students are New York–bred lovers of hip-hop. Around five years ago, I noticed that my kids were beginning to wear those white Lance Armstrong–style wristbands that say, "I Love Hip-Hop." Their love for hip-hop, interestingly, didn't know what to do with Southern hip-hop or Mississippi. They didn't love the South or Southern hip-hop, and they weren't sure that most Southern artists hadn't stylized their Southern worlds into digestible, aesthetically acceptable terms for "real lovers" of New York hip-hop.

They were equally unsure how to deal with the fact that the South began to sell millions more albums and get way more spins than any other region in the country, while newish New York hip-hop created a number of young artists who actually sounded Southern. So many of my students, like many other so-called purists, dismissed Southern hip-hop as ignorant, catchy, pop, hollow, shameful. Most of my students knew, and wanted me to believe, that in addition to white suburbia's uncritical devouring of the music minus culture and the countless emcees pandering to the Black girl audience in the hallway and corporate America's glossy detailing of hip-hop, the music was dying because Three 6 Mafia won an Oscar, Trina showed her booty, Mike Jones went platinum, Lil Jon couldn't rap, and Trinidad James was Trinidad James.

I honestly didn't see any of this coming in that Central Mississippi B-Boy bathroom twenty years ago, but I did understand that loving New York hip-hop wasn't enough. Isolated from caring and curious Black girls in the hallway and a destructive white gaze in my Central Mississippi world, I loved New York and New York hip-hop through the likes of Kane, KRS, Rakim, and LL. But even in that safe space, in longing for hip-hop and loving what B. Dazzle represented, I couldn't fully love my Southern self, Southern Black girls, or the culture that created us.

The raggedy clinking of this essay should not contradict

the fact that we Southern Black Boys and girls owe New York an almost unpayable debt. New York hip-hop literally gave us means to boast, critique, and confess ourselves into a peculiar existence, in ciphers and on the page. And really, it let us love its brilliance. For that, I will always respect New York ciphers, aesthetics, and sounds.

It's taken me twenty years to understand why my uttering and writing the word "cipher" frightened me for so long. The "cipher" reminded me of the Southern Black Boy who longed, like Lil Wayne, Jay Electronica, and J. Cole a few years ago, for an artistic letter of acceptance from New York. Truth be told, the art of Big K.R.I.T., Charlie Braxton, Cassandra Wilson, Richard Wright, and Margaret Walker Alexander helped me reckon with a fear that my work would never be significant without a stylization that accommodated what I believed were New York sensibilities.

I now accept the Black Boys, Invisible Men, Native Sons, and Blues People who grandfolked hip-hop into existence. And just like its grandfolks, I also accept that while it's painfully brilliant, innovative, and inspiring at times, hip-hop hasn't come close to meaningfully loving, accepting, and disagreeing with Black women and girls; it's kept their sensibilities, ears, eyes, and voices in the hallway and/or pandered to what we believe is their pussies, instead of asking and imagining what's happening in their ciphers. It also hasn't come close to faithfully disarming and laughing at white gazes. Nor has it even come close to gracefully mediating the space between the urban and the rural, the gaps between poverty and working poor, the difference between new money and wealth. And though it's come closer to realizing and illuminating these relationships in more considerable ways than contemporary literature, punditry, television, movies, or any mass of critical citizenry, it probably never will.

But if it can't do these things, or we can't do these things through hip-hop, from what are we running when we proclaim a love for hip-hop? That's the question. In and out of B-Boy ciphers, Black Boys like me have been asking a music and a so-called culture, as hokey as it sounds, to do the real work of the self, and the soul—really, work that Black Southerners have been doing for decades.

We Black Southerners, through life, love, and labor, are the generators and architects of American music, narrative, language, capital, and morality. That belongs to us. Take away all those stolen West African girls and boys forced to find an oral culture to express, resist, and signify in the South, and we have no rich American idiom. Erase Nigger Jim from our literary imagination and we have no American story of conflicted movement, place, and moral conundrum. Eliminate the Great Migration of Southern Black girls and boys and you have no Los Angeles, Chicago, Detroit, Indianapolis, Cleveland, or New York City. Expunge the sorrow songs, gospel, and blues of the Deep South and we have no rock and roll, rhythm and blues, funk, or hip-hop.

I am a Black Southern artist. Our tradition is responsible for me, and I am responsible to it.

When OutKast won the *Source* magazine's "Best New Artist" award more than ten years ago at the Apollo, New York booed. Andre 3000 addressed the booing of "them closed-minded folks" with the defiant utterance that "the South got something to say and that's all I got to say." Up until this very point, I've agreed with Andre to death and hoped to God he was right. I now know that he was and he wasn't. The South not only has something to say to New York; it has something to say to itself and to the world, and we've been saying it for years, decades, centuries. As hip-hop has grown way bigger than New York, and the new sound and art coming from New

York ciphers and writerly circles have become more mimetic and less soulfully significant, New York and the rest of the country now has to listen, take note, and literally emulate us, even if they still don't fully respect or understand from whence we come.

It's okay.

I'm not sure that what deeply southern artists are saying today is the most meaningful work in the world. I know that it is the most meaningful work in *my* world. And without the historic and contemporary sounds, sayings, and doings of Imani Perry, Sarah Broom, Maurice Ruffin, Derrick Harriell, Jesmyn Ward, C. Liegh McInnis, Eddie Glaude, Charlie Braxton, Zandria Robinson, K.R.I.T., Jamey Hatley, Angie Thomas, Crooked Lettaz, Aunjanue Ellis, and Natasha Trethewey, American art would be sleek, conventional, heady, pallid, and paltry as the blank piece of paper on the last page of this book, and probably just as hollow as the center of the next cipher.

Shh . . . listen. Go ahead and listen hard. Does that sound blue to you?

It don't even matter no more, cousin. We hear us. We hear you, too. Exactly. And that's all I should have ever had to say about that.

OUR KIND
OF RIDICULOUS

When I was twenty-four, I flew paper airplanes past the apartment of a thirty-two-year-old white boy named Trimp in Emmaus, Pennsylvania. Trimp rocked a greasy brown mullet, bragged about ironing his bleached Lee's, and said the word "youse" a lot. Even with caked-up cornbread sealing the cracks of his teeth and a raggedy mustache that looked like it was colored by a hyper six-year-old, Trimp always reminded me of somebody cute.

Trimp, whose apartment was directly above mine, lived with two women. One was his girlfriend. She could see. One was his wife. She could not.

Three little boys lived in the apartment with Trimp and his two partners. The youngest boy was Trimp's girlfriend's child. This miniature Viking loved to run his muddy hands through his blond hair and grin when he wasn't growling. The other two boys looked like they rolled around naked in a tub of melted Tootsie Rolls before coming out to play.

I was in Pennsylvania working on my graduate thesis while Nicole, my girlfriend at the time, interned at Rodale Press. Though I had spent most of my life in Mississippi, close to Black folks who were thirty cents away from a quarter, that summer in Emmaus, Pennsylvania, was the most intimate I'd ever been with white folks who barely had a pot to piss in.

After paying our rent, food, and utilities, Nicole and I had about $140 left in disposable income every month.

That $140 had me feeling quite bougie.

It was the first summer I hadn't worked as a phone book deliveryman, a waiter at Ton-o-Fun, a health care assistant at Grace House, a knife salesman at Cutco, a bootleg porter at the Buie House, a counselor at Upward Bound, or a summer school teacher at Indiana University. I was on a fellowship, which meant for the first time in my life, my job was simply to collect a small check in exchange for not wasting reading's and writing's time.

During the day, when I wasn't reading and writing, I made paper airplanes and talked outside with Shay, our eight-year-old neighbor; Barry, her six-year-old brother; and Trimp's kids. For most of the summer, Trimp's kids looked into our empty apartment through a huge sliding glass door. At first, they would stand about a foot from the door, looking directly at their reflections and our empty living room. A week or so into the summer, all three of Trimp's kids started smashing their faces against the door and running their muddy hands up and down the glass.

Shay and Barry had what Grandmama called good home-training. They simply watched Trimp's kids watch us from a distance and whispered in each other's ears.

Our apartment held one chair, one desk, a blow-up bed, a fridge covered in word magnets, and a cranky Mac. While Trimp's place smelled like fried meats, thin gravy, sticky fruit punches, and nappy carpet that rarely got vacuumed, our place smelled like new paint and feet. *Miseducation*, *ATLiens*, *Aquemini*, and the greatest hits of Joni Mitchell and Curtis Mayfield worked to shield our ears from Trimp's mash-up of Zeppelin, short-people screams, laughter, and that gotdamn Cartoon Network.

One July weekend, someone got shot in the building next to ours. As soon as the police left, Trimp and I walked over to see what we could.

As we walked, Trimp asked me how to pronounce my name. He'd heard his kids call me "Keith" and Nicole call me "Key" or "Kiese."

After I told him that Keith was fine, he asked me if he could borrow ten dollars. I told him I'd give it to him when we got back to our building.

Trimp and I kept walking and talking about his odd family arrangement and money a little while longer before he asked me if people got shot a lot where I was from.

I stopped to look him in the eye and see if he was asking a question he really wanted answered.

He wouldn't look back.

I didn't tell Trimp anything about missing Mississippi, or how I was reckoning with the fact that a friend of mine had taken a young woman into the Central Mississippi woods, blown her brains out, and was now serving a life sentence. I ignored Trimp's question completely and asked him about Pennsylvania amusement parks, Italian ices, and when he planned on getting a job.

After he answered all my questions, Trimp got really close to my face. He looked up at me and didn't run from my eyes. "Keith, youse should move here," he said. "I'm serious. Youse are different. Youse ain't like your kind."

He kept saying it, too, absolutely sure he'd given me that *gift* that a number of white folks I'd met loved to give Black folks at the strangest times, the *gift* of being decidedly different than all them other niggers. It felt like Trimp wanted a pat on the back for not saying the word "nigger," two pats for distinguishing one nigger from another nigger, and three pats for inching closer to the realization that Black Americans were never niggers to begin with.

On the way back from the murder site, Trimp walked ahead of me. I gripped his bony shoulder before we got to the hill leading up to our building. I asked him if his greasy mullet, his two in-house partners, his caved-in chest, his white BéBé's kids, and his belief in niggers made him different than his kind.

"I ain't racist, Keith," he kept saying.

"That's sweet," I told him.

Trimp wiggled free of my grip and walked up the hill to our building. I caught up with him outside of our glass door. I told him that the problem was that the niggers he believed in knew so much more about his kind than even he did, and that the niggers he believed in were taught to never ever be surprised by the slick shit that came out of the mouths of white folks. Then I got all graduate school on him and spouted some mess about dissonance, dissemblance, white absolution, and how it might be impossible for him to know if I was different than my kind if he didn't know himself.

Trimp turned his back on me and my big words.

He walked upstairs to his family and slammed his door. I walked into our empty apartment, partly disappointed that I didn't slap the taste out of Trimp's mouth and mostly ashamed that there was so much more I wanted to say to him.

If white American entitlement meant anything, it meant that no matter how patronizing, unashamed, deliberate, unintentional, poor, rich, rural, urban, ignorant, and destructive white Americans were, Black Americans were still encouraged to work for them, write to them, listen to them, talk with them, run from them, emulate them, teach them, dodge them, and ultimately thank them for not being as fucked up as they could be.

That's part of what I learned in Emmaus, Pennsylvania.

Trimp avoided me the rest of the summer, but his kids still banged their muddy hands on our sliding glass door every morning. A few days after Trimp said I was different than my kind, his youngest child walked into our apartment and started playing with the word magnets on our refrigerator. I placed the words "wash" "your" "dirty" "face" "and" "hands" "sometimes" "boy" in a line and asked him to read that sentence.

Trimp's son looked at the words, moved them around, smiled, and clapped his muddy hands like he was lightweight touched before proudly saying, "Nope. I can't even read, Keith. Nope. I can't. I can't even read!" The little muddy joker said it the way you would expect a white child to say, "Gee! I found the treasure. Yep! I really found the treasure."

I laughed in that child's face for a good minute and a half.

Deep. Terrible. Evil. Sad laughs.

And he laughed back, thinking I was laughing with him.

For worse—never better—nothing I saw, or heard, or smelled, or touched, or felt from Trimp and his family surprised me that summer.

I cannot say the same about myself.

A month or so after I laughed at that little boy's illiteracy, two of Nicole's friends came to visit. I don't remember much about Nicole's friends except one of them was the roundest short adult I'd ever met and she tried too hard not to sound like she was from rural West Virginia. Every few seconds, she managed to throw the words "ridiculous" and "totally" into something that wasn't ridiculous or totally anything.

Nicole drove a tiny green Geo Metro that I couldn't drive because it was a stick, and also because my license was suspended. The four of us piled in that Geo and headed to a Lilith Fair concert in Hershey. The concert wasn't Fresh Fest, and I didn't love the wet fog of patchouli and weed, or the lack of my kind at the show, but it ended up making me smile and feel a lot.

After the concert, we stopped at a gas station before leaving Hershey and heading back to Emmaus. A few minutes after we got on the interstate, I reminded Nicole to turn on her headlights.

Seconds later, we heard the siren.

A young white cop came to Nicole's side and pointed his flashlight at me in the passenger seat. I asked him if I could open the glove compartment to get her registration. He told me to keep my hands in plain sight.

I laughed at him. "See?" I said to Nicole.

An older white cop came up from behind us and approached my side. Both cops walked to the front of the Geo, talked for a second, then told me to get out of the car.

"For what?" I asked, now fake-laughing.

"Because we saw you throw crack out of the window."

I sucked my teeth. "I don't even drink or eat meat," I told the cop. *I don't even drink or eat meat?*

I pointed toward the field and told both cops again that I didn't throw crack out of the car and that we could all go look if they wanted to.

When I raised my arms, the bigger cop put his hands on his gun and told me to put my hands on the car. He patted me down and handcuffed me while Nicole watched from the driver's side and her ridiculous round friend sat quietly in the back of the car talking to the girl whose voice I can't even remember.

Blackness is probable cause, I tell myself.

I'm handcuffed in front of the flashing blue lights of a parked police car and a green Geo Metro. I've had guns pulled on me before and I was never afraid.

This is different.

The handcuffs hurt more than the thought of bullets. The two cops with deep frown lines place me in the back of the police car "for my own good" as a parade of mostly drunk white folks, on their way home from Lilith Fair, drive down the highway looking in our direction.

Humiliation.

I am guilty of being too much like my kind, which means I am one mistaken movement from being a justifiable homicide, or a few planted rocks from being incarcerated.

This is American law. In Hershey. In Jackson. In Indiana. In Ohio. In Minnesota. In Louisville.

This is American life.

But another kind of American law is happening to the women I was driving with in the Geo.

Two cops are touching the women in ways that they would never touch me. They are watching their bodies in ways they never watch mine. They are talking down to them in tones that say I want the chance to fuck you, and if you don't give me that chance to fuck you, I want the chance to fuck you up. The cops laugh and smirk whenever the women say anything. I'm watching the police search Nicole's car. They pull out a backpack from the trunk. The older cop reaches in the backpack and grabs what looks like the condoms they gave out at Lilith Fair. He holds the backpack up in the face of the women and shakes his head.

This is American life.

I'm wondering what will happen if I kick open the door and ask the cops, "Remember Tang? Can I pour a whole container of dry Tang down your throat until you throw up and your uniform is covered in thick dark orange Tang? It'll look like blood. It won't tastes like blood, though."

It will not taste like blood.

I'm wondering if Nicole, who is now standing at the back of her green Geo Metro talking to one of the cops, will think I could have actually thrown crack out of her passenger-side window.

I'm wondering if Nicole is wondering if she ever really knew me.

From the backseat of the police car, I'm watching this blinking blue field where my kind has thrown lots of invisible, and not so invisible, rocks of crack. I convince myself that Mississippi is on the other side of that field.

I want to run to Mississippi.

For a second, though—truth be told—I'm wondering if I actually did throw crack out of the window. Sitting in the back of that police car in handcuffs that have been wrapped around the wrists of many of my kind, I'm wondering if there's any chance that I am what, not who, they think I am.

One of the cops comes to the back of the police car I'm sitting in and tells me to get out.

"Thought you said we wouldn't find anything in your bag," he says, shaking a pack of condoms in my face.

As calm as I can, still water cradling my eyes, I say, "You should find that crack you saw me throw or you should let me go." The cop makes some comment about my mouth and takes the handcuffs off.

I want to run to Mississippi.

"All the people that you could've stopped, and you chose us?" I say with my hands pressed against my thighs. Cars filled with white folks keep passing us. They're all watching, mostly knowing what my kind is capable of. I wonder if Trimp is in one of those cars. I wonder, too, how many of my kind saw me handcuffed on the side of the road that night.

"You'uns safe tonight," the older officer says. "We're just doing our job."

"That was so ridiculous," Nicole's friend keeps saying from the backseat as we head home. "That was so totally ridiculous."

No one else is saying a word. Nicole is driving eight miles per hour below the speed limit.

As we get closer to Emmaus, Nicole's friend starts replaying what happened from the beginning of the concert to the cops saying I threw crack out the window.

She nervously says "totally" and "ridiculous" a few more times. She never says "afraid," "angry," "worried," "complicit," "tired," or "ashamed."

I do not understand why.

We got out of the Geo and saw the blue flickering of the TV on the upstairs balcony of Trimp's apartment. Trimp and his family were watching something with a loud laugh track. Our sliding glass door was covered in new muddy smudges.

I walked into the smaller bedroom of our apartment. While Nicole's friend kept replaying what happened for the third time in the living room, I dug my feet into the carpet of the bedroom and tried to push myself through the wall.

Nicole knocked on the door.

"You OK?" she asked me.

"I'm good," I said. "For real. You should spend some time with your friends before they leave. Are you okay?"

Nicole looked at me like she wanted to say everything was going to be okay. I wanted her to say that we were the collateral damage of a nation going through growing pains. Part of me wanted us to hug and agree each other to death that we were better people than we actually were. Nicole kept staring at me through the silence when we heard some thumping and screaming upstairs. I told her that I was sorry for being a dick, but I just wanted to read and write before going to bed.

I grabbed my notebook and told myself I was going to use that day as fuel to finish a chapter I was writing about four kids from Mississippi who time-travel through a hole in the ground. The kids think time-travel is the only way to make their state and their nation love itself and the kids coming after them. I scribbled away at a chapter before getting stuck on these two sentences one of the characters sees written in sawdust in a work shed around 1964:

We are real Black characters with real character, not the stars of American racist spectacle. Blackness is not probable cause.

We are real Black characters with real character, not the stars of American racist spectacle. Blackness is not probable cause.

We are real Black characters with real character, not the stars of American racist spectacle. Blackness is not probable cause.

We are real Black characters . . .

After what happened that day, all that really mattered was making it to those two clunky sentences. Everything else, for better and worse, including Trimp's intentions, the nasty work of the police, and all of our shame, was as light as the paper airplanes I threw past Trimp's apartment. And making it to that point, as quiet as it's kept, felt like the most that one of my kind could ask for, a few minutes from some invisible crack, not that many miles from central Mississippi, and directly beneath the apartment of an American white boy from Emmaus who needed to say "your kind" way more than an' one of y'all could ever imagine.

HOW TO SLOWLY
KILL YOURSELF AND
OTHERS IN AMERICA

I've had guns pulled on me by four people under Central Mississippi skies—once by a white undercover cop, once by a young brother trying to rob me for the leftovers of a weak work-study check, once by my mother, and twice by myself. Not sure how or if I've helped many folks say yes to life, but I've definitely aided in a few folks dying slowly in America, all without the aid of a gun.

I'm seventeen, five years younger than Rekia Boyd will be when she is shot in the head by an off-duty police officer in Chicago in 2012. It's the summer after I graduated high school, and my teammate, Troy, is back in Jackson, Mississippi. Troy, who plays college ball in Florida, asks me if I want to go to McDonald's on I-55.

As Troy, Cleta, Leighton, and I walk out of McDonald's, I hold the door open for a tiny, scruffy-faced white man with a green John Deere hat on.

"Thanks, partner," he says.

A few minutes later, we're driving down I-55 when John Deere drives up and lowers his window. I figure that he wants to say something funny since we'd had a cordial moment at McDonald's. As soon as I roll my window down, the man screams "Nigger lovers!" and speeds off.

On I-55, we pull up beside John Deere and I'm throwing finger-signs, calling John Deere all kinds of clever "motherfuckers." The dude slows down and gets behind us. I turn around, hoping he pulls over.

Nope.

John Deere pulls out a police siren and places it on top of his car. Troy is cussing my ass out and frantically trying to drive his mama's Lincoln away from John Deere. My heart is pounding out of my chest—not out of fear, but because I want a chance to choke the shit out of John Deere. I can't think of any other way of making him feel what we felt.

Troy drives into his apartment complex and parks his mama's long Lincoln under some kind of shed. Everyone in the car is slumped down at this point. Around twenty seconds after we park, here comes the red, white, and blue of the siren.

We hear a car door slam, then a loud knock on the back window. John Deere has a gun in one hand and a badge in the other. He's telling me to get out of the car. My lips still smell like Filet-O-Fish grease.

"Only you," he says to me. "You going to jail tonight." He's got the gun to my chest.

"Fuck you," I tell him and suck my teeth. "I ain't going nowhere."

I don't know what's wrong with me.

Cleta is up front trying to reason with the man through her window when all of a sudden, in a scene straight out of *Boyz n the Hood*, a Black cop approaches the car and accuses us of doing something wrong. Minutes later, a white cop tells us that John Deere has been drinking too much, and he lets us go.

Sixteen months later, I'm eighteen, three years older than Edward Evans will be when he is shot in the head behind an abandoned home in Jackson in 2012.

Nzola and I are walking from Subway back to Millsaps

College with two of her white friends. It's nighttime. We have turned off North State Street and walked halfway past the cemetery when a red Corolla filled with Black boys stops in front of us. All of the boys have blue rags covering their noses and mouths. One of the boys, a kid at least two years younger than me with the birdest of bird chests, gets out of the car clutching a shiny silver gun.

He comes toward Nzola and me.

"Me," I say to him. "Me. Me." I hold my hands up, encouraging him to do whatever he needs to do. If he shoots me, well, I guess bullets enter and hopefully exit my chest, but if he thinks I'm getting pistol-whupped in front of a cemetery and my girlfriend off State Street, I'm convinced I'm going to take the gun and beat him into a cinnamon roll.

The boy places his gun on my chest and keeps looking back and forth to the car.

I feel a strange calm, an uncanny resolve. I don't know what's wrong with me. He's patting me down for money that I don't have, since we hadn't gotten our work-study checks yet and I had just spent my last little money on two turkey subs and two of those large chocolate chip cookies.

The young brother keeps looking back to the car, unsure what he's supposed to do. Nzola and her friends are screaming when he takes the gun off my chest and trots goofily back to the car.

I don't know what's wrong with him, but a few months later, I have a gun.

A partner of mine hooks me up with a partner of his who lets me hold something. I get the gun not just to defend myself from goofy brothers in red Corollas trying to rob folks for work-study money. I guess I'm working on becoming a Black writer in Mississippi and some folks around Millsaps College don't like the essays I'm writing in the school newspaper.

A few weeks earlier, George Harmon, the president of Millsaps, shut down the campus paper in response to a satirical essay I wrote on communal masturbation and sent a letter to more than twelve thousand overwhelmingly white Millsaps students, friends, and alumnae. The letter stated that the "key essay in question was written by Kiese Laymon, a controversial writer who consistently editorializes on race issues."

After the president's letter goes out, my life kinda hurts.

I receive a sweet letter in the mail with the burnt-up ashes of my essays. The letter says that if I don't stop writing and give myself "over to right," my life will end up like the ashes of my writing.

The tires of my mama's car are slashed when it was left on campus. I'm given a single room after the dean of students thinks it's too dangerous for me to have a roommate. Greg Miller, a professor who teaches me to love Shakespeare, has a student in his liberal arts class say, "Kiese should be killed for what he's writing." Greg crafts an essay supportive of my right to create satirical critiques of the violent civility Millsaps and its Greek culture encourage. I am thankful for Greg's support, but I don't know what's wrong with me.

It's Bid Day at Millsaps.

Nzola and I are headed to our jobs at Ton-o-Fun, a fake-ass Chuck E. Cheese behind Northpark Mall. We're wearing royal-blue shirts with a strange smiling animal and "Ton-o-Fun" on the left titty. The shirts of the other boy workers at Ton-o-Fun fit them better than mine fits me. My shirt is tight in the wrong places and slightly less royal-blue. I like to add a taste of bleach so I don't stank.

As we walk out to the parking lot of my dorm, the Kappa Alpha and Kappa Sigma fraternities are in front of the dorm receiving their new members. They've been up drinking all night. Some of them have on blackface and others have on Afro wigs and Confederate capes.

128

We get close to Nzola's Saturn and one of the men says, "Kiese, write about this!" Then another voice calls me a "nigger" and Nzola a "nigger b—." I think and feel a lot, without thinking or feeling much at all about the content of Nzola's fear, but mostly I feel that I can't do anything to make the boys feel like they've made me feel right there, so I go back to my dorm room to get something.

On the way there, Nzola picks up a glass bottle out of the trash. I tell her to wait outside the room. I open the bottom drawer and look at the hoodies balled up on top of my gun. I pick up my gun and think about my Grandmama. I think not only about what she'd feel if I went back out there with a gun. I think about how if Grandmama walked out of that room with a gun in hand, she'd use it. No question.

I am her grandson.

I throw the gun back on top of the clothes, close the drawer, go in my closet, and pick up a wooden T-ball bat.

Some of the KAs and Sigs keep calling us names as we approach them. I step, throw down the bat, and tell them I don't need a bat to fuck them up. I don't know what's wrong with me. My fists are balled up and the only thing I want in the world is to swing back over and over again. Nzola feels the same, I think. She's right in the mix, yelling, crying, fighting as best she can. After security and a dean break up the mess, the frats go back to receiving their new pledges and Nzola and I go to work at Ton-o-Fun in our dirty blue shirts.

I stank.

On our first break at work, we decide that we should call a local news station so the rest of Jackson can see what's happening at Millsaps on a Saturday morning. We meet the camera crew at school. Some of boys go after the reporter and cameraman. The camera gets a few students in Afros, blackface, and Confederate capes. They also get footage of "another altercation."

A few weeks pass and George Harmon, the president of the college, doesn't like that this footage of his college is now on television and in newspapers all across the country. The college decides that two individual fraternity members, Nzola, and I will be put on disciplinary probation for using "racially insensitive language" and that the two fraternities involved will get their party privileges taken away for a semester. If there was racially insensitive language Nzola and I could have used to make those boys feel like we felt, we would have never stepped to them in the first place. Millsaps is trying to prove to the nation that it is a post-race(ist) institution and to its alums that all the Bid Day stuff is the work of an "adroit entrepreneur of racial conflict," as I am called in a letter to the editor in the *Clarion Ledger*.

Nzola and I continue to hurt each other because I refuse to practice the Black feminist theory I read. My response, stated and unstated, to her reckoning with what she experienced as the only Black woman in a quad of drunk white men and one obsessed Black man is, "You don't know what it's like to be hunted as a Black man."

Nzola lets me know, in every way she can, that I am a typical Black man with just a few more words at my disposal. This, she says, actually makes me more dangerous than an ignorant fucking KA. I laugh when Nzola says that.

I don't know what's wrong with me.

A few months later, Mama and I sit in President George Harmon's office. The table is an oblong mix of mahogany and ice water. All the men at the table are smiling, flipping through papers, and twirling pens in their hands except for me. I am still nineteen, four years older than Hadiya Pendleton will be when she is murdered in Chicago.

President Harmon and his lawyers don't look me in the eye. They zero in on the eyes of Mama, as Harmon tells her that I am being suspended from Millsaps for at least a year for tak-

130

ing and returning *The Red Badge of Courage* from the library without formally checking it out.

He ain't lying.

I took the book out of the library for Nzola's brother without checking it out and I returned it the next day. I looked right at the camera when I did it, too. I did all of this knowing I was on parole, but not believing any college in America, even one in Mississippi, would kick a student out for a year for taking and returning a library book without properly checking it out.

I should have believed.

George Harmon tells me, while looking at my mother, that I will be allowed to come back to Millsaps College in a year only after having attended therapy sessions for racial insensitivity. We are told he has given my writing to a local psychologist and the shrink believes I need help. Even if I am admitted back as a student, I will remain formally on parole for the rest of my undergrad career, which means that I will be expelled from Millsaps College unless I'm perfect.

Nineteen-year-old Black boys cannot be perfect in America. Neither can sixty-year-old white boys named George.

Before riding home with Mama, I go to my room, put the gun in my backpack, and get in her car.

On the way home, Mama stops by the zoo to talk about what just happened in George Harmon's office. She's crying and asking me over and over again why I took and returned the gotdamn book knowing they were watching me. Like a loving Black mother of her only Black boy, Mama starts blaming Nzola for asking me to check the book out in the first place. I don't know what to say other than that I knew it wasn't Nzola's fault and that I left my ID behind and I didn't want to swing back to get it, so I kept walking and said nothing. She says that Grandmama is going to be so disappointed in me.

"Heartbroken" is the word she uses.

There.

I feel this toxic miasma unlike anything I've ever felt, not just in my body, but in my blood. I remember the wobbly way my Grandmama twitches her eyes at my uncle Jimmy, and I imagine being at the end of that twitch for the rest of my life. For the first time in almost two years, I hide my face, grit my crooked teeth, and sob.

I don't stop for weeks.

The NAACP and lawyers get involved in filing a lawsuit against Millsaps on my behalf. Whenever the NAACP folks talk to me or to the newspaper, they talk about how ironic it is that a Black boy trying to read a book gets kicked out of college. I appreciate their work, but I don't think the irony lies where they think it does. If I'd never read a book in my life, I shouldn't have been punished that way for taking and bringing back a library book—not when kids are smoking that good stuff, drinking themselves unconscious, and doing some of everything imaginable to nonconsenting bodies.

That's what I tell all the newspapers and television reporters who ask. To my friends, I say that after stealing all those Lucky Charms, Funyuns, loaves of light bread, and over a hundred cold dranks out of the cafeteria in two years, how in the fuck do I get suspended for taking and returning the gotdamn *Red Badge of Courage*?

The day I'm awarded the Benjamin Brown Award, named after a twenty-one-year-old truck driver shot in the back by police officers during a student protest near Jackson State in 1967, I take the bullets out of my gun, throw it in the Ross Barnett Reservoir, and avoid Grandmama and Nzola.

I don't know what's wrong with me.

I enroll at Jackson State University, where my mother teaches political science, in the spring semester. Even though I'm not really living at home, Mama and I fight every day over

132

my job at Cutco and her staying with her boyfriend and her not letting me use the car to get to my second job at an HIV hospice since my license is suspended.

Really, we're fighting because she raised me to never ever forget I was born on parole, which means no black hoodies in wrong neighborhoods, no jogging at night, hands in plain sight at all times in public, no intimate relationships with white women, never driving over the speed limit or doing those rolling stops at stop signs, always speaking the King's English in the presence of white folks, never being outperformed in school or in public by white students, and, most important, always remembering that no matter what, *the worst of white folks* will do anything to get you.

Mama's antidote to being born a Black boy on parole in Central Mississippi is not for us to seek freedom, but to insist on excellence at all times. Mama takes it personal when she realizes that I realize she is wrong. There ain't no antidote to life, I tell her. How free can you be if you really accept that white folks are the traffic cops of your life? Mama tells me that she is not talking about freedom. She says that she is talking about survival.

One blue night Mama tells me that I need to type the rest of my application to Oberlin College after I've already handwritten the personal essay. I tell her that it doesn't matter whether I type it or not since Millsaps is sending a dean's report attached to my transcript. I say some other truthful things I should never say to my mother. Mama goes into her room, lifts up her pillow, and comes out with her gun.

It's raggedy, small, heavy, and black, like a crow. I'd held it a few times before with Mama hiding behind me and a friend of hers around the corner.

Mama points the gun at me and tells me to get the fuck out of her house. I look right at the muzzle pointed at my face and

133

smile the same way I did at the library camera at Millsaps. I don't know what's wrong with me.

"You gonna pull a gun on me over some college application?" I ask her.

"You don't listen until it's too late," she tells me. "Get out of my house and don't ever come back."

I leave the house chuckling, shaking my head, cussing under my breath. I go sit in a shallow ditch. Outside, I wander in the topsy-turvy understanding that Mama's life does not revolve around me and that I'm not doing anything to make her life more joyful, spacious, or happy. I'm an ungrateful burden, an obese weight on her already terrifying life. I sit there in the ditch, knowing that other things are happening in my mother's life, but also knowing that Mama never imagined needing to pull a gun on the child she carried on her back as a sophomore at Jackson State. I'm playing with pine needles, wishing I had headphones—but mostly I'm regretting throwing my gun into the reservoir.

When Mama leaves for work in the morning, I break back into her house, go under her pillow, and get her gun. Mama and I haven't paid the phone or the light bill, so it's dark, hot, and lonely in that house, even in the morning. I lie in a bathtub of cold water, still sweating, and singing love songs to myself.

I put the gun to my forehead and cock it.

I think of my Grandmama and remember that old feeling of being so in love that nothing matters except seeing and being seen by her. I drop the gun to my chest. I'm so sad and I can't really see a way out of what I'm feeling but I'm leaning on memory for help. Faster. Slower. I think I want to hurt myself more than I'm already hurting. I'm not the smartest boy in the world by a long shot, but even in my funk I know that easy remedies like eating your way out of sad, or fucking your way out of sad, or lying your way out of sad, or slanging your way out of sad, or robbing your way out of sad, or gambling your way out of sad, or shooting your way out of sad, are just slower, more acceptable ways for desperate folks, and especially paroled Black boys in our country, to kill ourselves and others close to us in America.

I start to spend more time at home over the next few weeks since Mama is out of town with her boyfriend. Mama and I still haven't paid the phone bill, so I'm running down to the pay phone every day, calling one of the admissions counselors at Oberlin College. He won't tell me whether they'll accept me or not, but he does say that Oberlin might want me because of, not in spite of, what happened at Millsaps.

A month passes and I haven't heard from Oberlin. I'm eating too much and dry-humping with a brilliant woman not named Nzola who is just as desperate as me. I'm lying like it's my first job, and daring people to fuck with me more than I have in a long time. I'm writing lots of words, too, but I'm not reckoning. I'm wasting ink on bullshit political analysis and short stories and vacant poems that I never imagine being read or felt by anyone like me. I'm an imitator, not a writer, and really, I'm a waste of writing's time.

The only really joyful times in life come from playing basketball and talking shit with O.G. Raymond "Gunn" Murph, my best friend. Gunn is trying to stop himself from slowly killing himself and others, after a smoldering breakup with V., his girlfriend of eight years. Some days, Gunn and I save each other's lives just by telling and listening to each other's odd-shaped truths.

One black night, Ray is destroying me in Madden and talking all that shit when we hear a woman moaning for help outside of his apartment on Capitol Street. We go downstairs and find a naked woman with open wounds, blood, and bruises all over her Black body. She can barely walk or talk through shivering teeth, but we ask her if she wants to come upstairs while we call the ambulance. Gunn and I have taken no sexual assault classes and we listen to way too much *The Diary* and *Ready to Die*, but right there, we know not to get too close to the woman and just let her know we're there to do whatever she needs.

She slowly makes her way into the apartment because she's afraid the men might come back. Blood is gushing down the back of her thighs and her scalp. She tells us the three men had one gun. When she makes it up to the apartment, we give the woman a brown towel to sit on and something to wrap herself in. Blood seeps through both and even though she looks so scared and hurt, she also looks so embarrassed. Gunn keeps saying things like, "It's gonna be okay, sweetheart," and I just sit there weakly nodding my head, running from her eyes and getting her more glasses of water. When Gunn goes in his room to take his gun out of his waistband, I look at her and know that no one man could have done this much damage to another human being.

That's what I need to tell myself.

Eventually, the ambulance and police arrive. They ask her a lot of questions and keep looking at us. She tells them that we helped her after she was beaten and raped by three Black men in a Monte Carlo. One of the men, she tells the police, was her boyfriend. She refuses to say his name to the police. Gunn looks at me and drops his eyes. Without saying anything, we know that whatever is in the boys in that car has to also be in us. We know that whatever is encouraging them to kill themselves slowly by knowingly mangling the body and spirit of this shivering Black girl, is probably the most powerful thing in our lives. We also wonder if whatever is in us that has been slowly encouraging us to kill ourselves is also in the heart and mind of the shivering Black girl on the couch.

A few weeks later, I get a letter saying I've been accepted

to Oberlin College and they're giving me a boatload of financial aid. Gunn agrees to drive me up to Oberlin and I feel like the luckiest boy on earth—not because I got into Oberlin, but because I survived long enough to remember to say "yes" to life and "no" or at least "slow down" to slow death.

My saying yes to life meant accepting the beauty of growing up Black, on parole, surrounded by a family of weird women warriors in Mississippi. It also meant accepting that George Harmon, parts of Millsaps College, parts of my state, much of my country, my heart, and mostly my own reflection, had beaten the dog shit out of me. I still don't know what all this means but I know it's true.

This isn't an essay or a woe-is-we narrative about how hard it is to be a Black boy in America. This is a lame attempt at remembering the contours of slow death and life in America for one Black American teenager under Central Mississippi skies. I wish I could get my Yoda on right now and sift all this into a clean sociopolitical pull-quote that shows supreme knowledge and absolute emotional transformation, but I don't want to lie.

I want to say that remembering starts not with predictable punditry, or bullshit blogs, or slick art that really asks nothing of us; I want to say that it starts with all of us willing ourselves to remember, tell, and accept those complicated, muffled truths of our lives and deaths, and the lives and deaths of folks all around us, over and over again.

Then I want to say that I am who Grandmama and Aunt Sue think I am.

I am not.

I'm a walking regret, a truth-teller, a liar, a survivor, a frowning ellipsis, a witness, a dreamer, a teacher, a student, a failure, a joker, a writer whose eyes stay red, and I'm a child of this nation.

I know that as I got deeper into my late twenties, and then my thirties, I managed to continue killing myself and other folks who loved me in spite of me. I know that I've been slowly killed by folks who were as feverishly in need of life and death as I am. The really confusing part is that a few of those folks who have nudged me closer to slow death have also helped me say yes to life when I most needed it. Usually, I didn't accept it. Lots of times, we've taken turns killing ourselves slowly, before trying to bring each other back to life.

By the time I left Mississippi, I was twenty years old, three years older than Trayvon Martin will be when he is murdered for wearing a hoodie and swinging back in the wrong American neighborhood. I am convinced I will never be a Black writer in America, because being the kind of Black writer in America I long to be gets you and people close to you hurt.

Four months after I leave Mississippi, San Berry, a twenty-year-old partner of mine who went to Millsaps College with Gunn and me, will be convicted for taking Pam McGill, an amazing social worker, into the woods, and shooting her in the head. San confesses to kidnapping Ms. McGill, driving her to some woods, making her fall to her knees, and pulling the trigger while a seventeen-year-old Black boy named Azikiwe waited for him in the car. San will eventually say that Azikiwe encouraged him to do it. I do not know what was wrong with San. Even today, journalists, activists, and others folks in Mississippi wonder what really happened with San, Azikiwe, and Pam McGill that day.

I can't front, though. I don't wonder about any of that. Not today.

I wonder what all three of those children of our nation really remembered about how to slowly kill themselves and other folks in America the day before parts of them lived, cried, and died under the blue-black sky in Central Mississippi.

THE WORST
OF WHITE FOLKS

Way back in the day, when Twitter was a bootleg reindeer name, David Rozier invented farting during Mass. A few minutes *before* we marveled at the six Catholics at Holy Family Catholic School sipping out of one gold goblet, and right *after* Father Joe suggested we offer each other "a sign of peace," David tapped me on my shoulder, swung his right arm around his back and farted in his hand. Father Joe rolled his eyes from the pulpit as David proceeded to shake the hands of Ms. Bockman, Ms. Raphael, and all the other sixth- and seventh-graders in our row.

Side by side, David and I looked as different as two Mississippi Black boys could look. He reminded me of a shorter version of my cousin Jermaine, who lived up in Chicago. David had the forearms and calves of a wiry point guard, with the teeniest head you'd ever seen in your life. He had bright, curious, clear eyes, a voice that was octaves deeper than you'd expect, and these elephant ears that Angela Williams would pluck on field trips. David wasn't the flyest dresser in the seventh grade, but he—like our boy Lerthon—came to school fabric-softener fresh with just a whiff of fried eggs and canned biscuits. I, on the other hand, was slightly less husky than the Human Beatbox and smelled like stale sweat and off-brand dishwashing soap.

The day David offered us his sign of peace, Ms. Bockman, who initially thought David was finally being respectful of Catholic tradition, went off on me in homeroom. When I wouldn't tell her why I was laughing, she walked me into the hallway and pointed down to the principal's office.

"Kiese, you're not giving me a choice," she said. "Move it!"

As I walked down the hall to the principal's office with Ms. Bockman at my side, our homeroom door opened behind us.

"Hold up!" It was David Rozier. "Kiese ain't do nothing," he told Ms. Bockman. "It's my bad he was laughing. I'm responsible."

I looked at David and waited for something more, something familiar.

I got nothing.

David just stood there swaying with his peanut head tucked into his chest. He wouldn't stop tracing the brown splotches on the floor with his toe.

Since fourth grade, David Rozier and I had spent every day calling and responding, daring each other to revise all the rules of Mississippi juvenile delinquency. We were the Run-DMC of bad behavior at Holy Family Catholic School, and Lerthon was our Jam Master Jay. But in that second, I was a spectator, a confused fan. Hard as I tried, I couldn't understand the movement, language, and work of American responsibility, especially coming from the mouth of David Rozier.

"I made Kiese laugh in Mass," David told Ms. Bockman.

"But you didn't laugh," she said.

"I passed gas in my hand and I spread it," I remember David saying without a smirk. I busted out laughing again. "Kiese wouldn't be laughing without me. I'm saying I'm responsible."

While we sat outside the principal's office waiting for the secretary to call our mamas, I joked that I saw Ms. Bockman smell her hand. David wouldn't laugh. After a minute or two of forced yawning to break the silence, I asked David why he'd accepted responsibility for my acting a fool.

"I don't even know," I remember him saying. "Coach Stanley said we gotta be more responsible for our team, and my Grandmama said I gotta start acting responsible, too. I forgot at first. Then I remembered."

I couldn't understand.

David and I got suspended from our rickety Black Catholic school that day. Later that evening, in our Black neighborhoods, our mothers called their mothers. Under our grandmothers' guidance, our backs, elbows, knees, necks, and thighs were destroyed. We now knew that the worst whupping you could get was the playing-fart-games-in-Catholic-church whupping. We figured it was our mothers' way of keeping us out of Black gangs, Black prisons, Black clinics, Black cemeteries. We knew it was their way of proving to our grandmothers that they were responsible.

The licks, during my whupping at least, were in sync with every syllable out of Mama's mouth.

At least twenty-five solid syllables. At least twenty-five stinging licks.

Near the second half of the whupping, Mama, who was usually reckless with her belt, channeled the precision of Grandmama and dropped ten licks to the words, "don't . . . you . . . know . . . white . . . folks . . . don't . . . care . . . if . . . you . . . die . . ."

Even as a juvenile delinquent who didn't fully understand what "responsibility" meant, I understood that when Mama said "white folks," she meant *the worst of white folks*. I knew this literally because there were so many different types of white folks on television, and the only white folks I knew personally at the time—Ms. Bockman, Ms. Jacoby, Ms. Raphael, and Lori Bakutis—were complicated, caring white folks who didn't want me dead. The truth was that you didn't have to know white folks personally to understand what *the worst of white folks* nudged your family to feel and do.

The worst of white folks, I understood, wasn't some gang of rabid white people in crisp pillowcases and shaved heads. *The worst of white folks* was a pathetic, powerful "it." It conveniently forgot that it came to this country on a boat, then reacted violently when anything or anyone suggested it share. *The worst of white folks* wanted our mamas and Grandmamas to work themselves sick for a tiny sliver of an American pie it needed to believe it had made from scratch. It was all at once crazy-making and quick to discipline us for acting crazy. It had an insatiable appetite for virtuoso Black performance and routine Black suffering. *The worst of white folks* really believed that the height of Black and brown aspiration should be emulation of itself. White Americans were wholly responsible for *the worst of white folks*, though they would make sure it never wholly defined them.

I didn't know a lot as a seventh-grader in Mississippi, and I had far fewer words to describe what I actually knew, but *the worst of white folks* I knew far too well. David Rozier and I both did.

It passed through blood.

Up in Maywood, Illinois, which is about ten miles west of downtown Chicago, my first cousin, Jermaine, was just as familiar with *the worst of white folks* as we were in Jackson. Though the winters were colder, the vowel sounds shorter, the buildings taller, and the yards a lot smaller, the Chicago I visited as a child always felt like an orange piece of Mississippi that had broken off and floated away, with one major exception.

Whereas the mid-twentieth century saw millions of Black Americans leave Alabama, Louisiana, and Mississippi for Chicago, Indianapolis, Milwaukee, Gary, and Detroit, by the mid-1980s we were in the midst of a much less concentrated reverse migration. Chicago's Vice Lords and Folks had made their way into Jackson and Memphis.

When David and I started the seventh grade, we heard rumors that rocking your hat tilted to the left or right, doing twisted things with your fingers, and wearing the wrong colors were grounds for a beatdown. But by the end of seventh grade, the rumors became full-fledged law in Jackson. As much as this law immediately altered the way David, Lerthon, Henry Wallace, and I moved through space near the end of seventh grade, this law sadly governed Jermaine's entire life in Chicago.

My father took me to visit my aunt, Jermaine, and his siblings the summer I turned fourteen. We didn't stay long, but the whole time I was there, I kept hoping that Jermaine would come back to stay with me in Jackson. I figured that girls like Marsha Middleton, who wouldn't give me much rhythm, would have to pay attention if they knew I was cool enough to have a cousin like Jermaine.

Jermaine carried himself like the quarterback Coach Stanley wanted Henry Wallace to become. It's crazy to say that you knew any boy or girl would grow up to become a leader of men and women, but you only had to watch how Jermaine patiently observed you with those clear, slow-blinking eyes to know that one day, he would be followed. We both walked the earth with clenched fists, but Jermaine's fists seemed more likely to open and offer you whatever you needed to get by.

Less than ten years after I visited my cousin in Chicago, Jermaine's little sister was murdered. Months later, Jermaine was incarcerated for manslaughter.

A little over a year ago, Jermaine got off probation, which meant he could finally leave Illinois. After exchanging a few texts about how sure he was Derrick Rose wouldn't let his Bulls fall to LeBron "KANG" James, Jermaine texted me, "Cuzzo I just want to be somewhere where I have some healthy choices. Can you help?" I texted him back, stating that I'd do whatever it took to get him and his little girls to New York so they all could breathe a different kind of air. I meant every word I texted, too.

Jermaine never asked me when he could come to New York. Instead, he sent periodic text messages praising his team, the Bulls, and questioning the bench production of my team, the Heat. "Win or go home, cuzzo" was his favorite text message. I'd get this text whenever his team played a great half or Rose bent laws of physics. Jermaine and I found joy in knowing that Black boys from places like Jackson and Chicago were using their athletic genius to obliterate expectations.

That was more than a year ago.

Jermaine is still in Illinois, piecing together work here and there, and I wake up every morning in a world distinguished by rolling hills, manicured meadows, potbellied squirrels, aged gnomes, and a make-out spot called Sunset Lake. Not only have I not sent for Jermaine and his family to join me, I haven't even asked him to come out for a weekend.

The worst of me, I understand, has less power than *the worst of white folks,* but morally is really no better. The worst of me wants credit for intending to do right by Jermaine, and has no intentions of disrupting my life for the needs of a cousin I always looked up to. I am no more equipped to use or understand the language and work of American responsibility as a grown-ass man than I was as a seventh-grader in the halls of Holy Family Catholic School.

A few years after David Rozier indirectly tried to show me the language and work of American responsibility, he and Henry Wallace were dead. The truth is that half the boys in that seventh-grade class at Holy Family died before reaching thirty-five years of age. I used to spend hours daydreaming about David, Henry, Roy Bennett, Tim Brown, Kareem Hill, and Jermaine while playing behind Lerthon's house. Roy, Tim,

Kareem, Jermaine, Lerthon and I were teenagers in my dream. David and Henry were not.

As our nation shamefully debated Chicago's murder rate during the summer of 2012, folding complicated human lives into convenient numbers that were shared, "liked," discussed, and neglected all around the country, I spent more time talking to Catherine Coleman, my grandmother.

I told her that I might attend this "Peace" basketball tournament in Chicago to promote an end to all the violence. I asked her what she thought of my inviting Jermaine to come with me.

Grandmama was quiet for a while. Then she asked me whether the Chicago mothers and grandmothers of kids living and dead would be attending the game.

"I don't know," I told her. "Probably some will."

"Tell those folks at the game that it would help to get the mamas and grandmamas there," she said. "And tell everybody watching them boys play ball that they need to listen to what the mamas and Grandmamas have to say."

It made too much sense.

Though my grandmother worked from the time she was seven years old, our nation forbade her from registering to vote until she was deep into her thirties. She has lived under American apartheid longer than she's been technically "free." Our nation told her she would enter the chicken plant as a line worker and retire as a line worker, no matter how well she worked. Our nation limited the amount of formal education she herself could attain and patted her on the back when she earned enough to buy her daughters and son a set of encyclopedias. Our nation watched her raise four Black children and two grandchildren to become teachers, all the while responsibly arming herself and her community against *the worst of white folks* and the destructive tendencies of neighbors.

Last month, after burying her brother, Rudy, Grandmama bent her knees and reckoned with burying her son, her sisters, her mother, her grandmother, her father, and all four of her best friends. She asked her God to spare her the responsibility of burying any more of her children or grandchildren. A few weeks later, an irresponsible American aspiring to be the leader of our nation, who got a majority of the vote from *the worst of white folks*, called her a "victim" who feels entitled to health care, food, and housing.

Catherine Coleman, along with my Grandmama Pudding, and David Rozier's grandmother, have never been allowed to just be victims. They're rarely even allowed to be Americans. They don't get invited to panel discussions. They aren't talked to by the DNC or RNC. No one asks them what to do about national violence, debt, or defense. They are not American superwomen, but they are the best of Americans. They have remained responsible, critical, and loving in the face of servitude, sexual assault, segregation, poverty, and psychological violence. They have done this hard, messy work because they were committed to life and justice, and so we all might live more responsibly tomorrow.

There is a price to pay for ducking responsibility, for clinging to the worst of us, for harboring a warped innocence. There is an even greater price to pay for ignoring, demeaning, and unfairly burdening those Americans who have disproportionately borne the weight of American irresponsibility for so long. Our grandmothers and great-grandmothers have paid more than their fair share, and our nation owes them and their children, and their children's children, a lifetime of healthy choices and second chances. That would be responsible.

• • •

When David Rozier came back to school the day after we were kicked out, he started playing this game where he would fart every time Henry mispronounced "strong" like "skrong," and "straight" like "skraight." David had me dying! I put my head down on my desk so I wouldn't get kicked out of school again and laughed into my forearm until I cried.

At recess, I asked David, "What happened to all that responsibility you were talking about?"

"Oh," he said and took off running a post pattern in the schoolyard. "Nigga, that was yesterday!"

I threw David a bomb, and as the ball half-spiraled through the air, neither one of us thought about tomorrow or yesterday. We were just so happy to be in the moment, so happy to be alive.

WE WILL NEVER
EVER KNOW

Dear Uncle Jimmy,

As a Black boy growing up in Mississippi, I learned that there was a rickety bridge between right and wrong. And I learned that I would be disciplined more harshly than white boys for even slightly leaning toward the wrong side. But like you, Uncle Jimmy, I sadly didn't give a fuck. I broke bets I made with myself, got kicked out of high school a number of times, was suspended from college, and had run-ins with police that broke Mama and Grandmama's heart. Unlike you, though, I did all of this in close proximity to a lanky, living, breathing warning.

Uncle Jimmy, that warning was you.

On July 4, you threw down your crack pipe, scrubbed yourself clean, and bought my Grandmama some meat. "This Mama's meat," you wrote in loopy black letters on a bloody paper sack. When your sister, my mama, called me in my office at Vassar in Poughkeepsie, New York, she had no idea that the Fourth of July would be the last day she would see you alive.

You joked with your sisters before taking little Tre to get more bottle rockets. Reeking of that familiar mix of sour scalp and Jordan cologne, you probably blinked those huge webbed eyes more than usual and actually asked questions of our family.

As with many of Mama's stories, you weren't the star, but you were the precocious, literally paroled man on whom our family's emotional stability truly rested. There was a terrible clarity in Mama's voice when she told me the story of July 4. Mama's voice sounded like this any time you followed a crack binge or a run-in with the police with something graceful like leading a Sunday school session or using your pension to buy that house over off Highway 35.

"You driving my sister crazy now," Aunt Sue told me, more than twenty years ago, the night I drove my mama into a nervous breakdown. "You heading down that same road as Jimmy."

I learned that night that the Uncle Jimmy road ran adjacent to the refined, curbed avenues that nearly all sisters, aunts, mamas, and Grandmamas want their Black boys to travel. Aunt Sue and Mama wanted me to know, without a doubt, that whatever consumed you would eventually consume me unless I prayed diligently, obeyed the law, remained clean, and got out of Mississippi by any means necessary. But even as I sprinted away from Mississippi to Ohio, then Indiana, and now New York, if I looked down I could never really distinguish your footprints from my own.

That's what I felt before July 7.

On July 7, three days after you toted that bag of meat to Grandmama's house, I got a call. Grandmama was looking for you. She drove over to your house because you wouldn't answer the phone. Grandmama opened the screen and pounded on your door that evening. She yelled your name over and over again, but you didn't answer.

You couldn't.

On July 12, eight days after you brought Grandmama her bloody meat, your sisters walked into Mapp Funeral Home and readied your body, the body of Grandmama's first child, and their only brother, for public viewing. My mama made the funeral director change your shirt.

Your sister Sue, the most mesmerizing preacher in Mississippi, eulogized you in Concord Baptist Church. We were all baptized there. At the core of Sue's eulogy were three ideas: (1) "Niggers" do not exist. (2) Perfectly sanitized, wholly responsible Black people do not exist. (3) You, Jimmy Alexander, were equally wicked and wonderful and had far more in common with us than we wanted to admit.

Aunt Sue made the church know that you lived a life of bad; not bad meaning good, or bad meaning evil, but bad meaning bad at being human. In traditional Old Testament style, she explored justice and recreated in you someone who had prepared himself for death by finally accepting and earning life in the days before your passing. Sue told the church the story of your bringing that meat to Grandmama's house. She told us that you had gotten your finances in order.

"Jimmy wasn't that different from anyone in this church," she told us. "No better or no worse. And that's what we have to accept. He was racing toward death, but he was a part of our family. He was all of our brother."

While Sue stood in the pulpit teaching us about acceptance of our badness, I realized that you were the only child of Grandmama's who did not become a teacher. If you had taught for a living, you might not have been any physically or emotionally healthier, since we know that occupations are never shields from reckless sex, drug abuse, cowardice, deceptiveness, and desperation. But Grandmama would have found far more peace on the day of your funeral if she had known her oldest child, a big-eyed Black boy born in the late 1940s, had taught somebody somewhere something before he died.

As Grandmama's youngest daughter gave the church words to lean on, your mother, our teacher, the thickest, most present human being either of us has known, folded up at the end of the pew. Grandmama cried herself breathless as your bloodless body lay right over the site of your baptism. I held Grand-mama, though, Uncle Jimmy. I held her just like she would have wanted you to hold her if I were stretched out in that casket.

I needed you, Uncle Jimmy. I needed you the day of your funeral. And when we were both alive, I needed you to be better than you were, but I never loved you enough to tell you. I could have shown you by calling you more, or walking with you down Old Morton Road when I visited during the summer and at Christmas. We could have wondered about the widened roads and the huge dying trees we both imagined fighting off Godzilla and Starscream. We could have joked and tossed ironic jabs back and forth as some nephews and uncles do.

Then, if we really cared, we could have harnessed the courage to knock each other's hustles.

I could have finally said, "Uncle Jimmy, you drowning yourself with that crack and all that hate. Ain't nothing really behind your smile, man. I love you and I need you to live." And you could have told me, "There's more than one way to drown, nephew. You looking pretty wet yourself. I know I'm under that water. You know where you at?"

But those words were never said. We talked, but we didn't reckon with each other. Hence, all of our communication created no meaningful reverberation outside our speculations about each other. The last thing you said to me the Christmas before you died was "No matter how much right you try to do, white folks do everything they can to make a nigga remember they owned us." There was a silence after that sentence, and I filled that silence with a mechanical nod of my head and a weak "Yeah. I hear that."

By that point, though, I believed I knew you. I assumed that you coped with the weight of a paroled life as a Black man in Mississippi by laughing, acting a fool, relying on crack cocaine, alcohol, and the manipulation of women who were just as hopeless as you. And I assumed that you knew that I'd started coping in many of the same ways. One of the only differences between you and me was that I fell deeply in love with the possibilities of written and spoken words. I used words to create stories, essays, and novels I thought you'd want to read, hear, and see. I never imagined I could make a life of writing, but I knew I'd always need writing to wander under and above life.

When I wasn't writing things that you might have wanted or needed to read, hear, and see, I created fictive versions of you that were, sadly, more interesting and more loving than I ever allowed you to be in real life. You inspired thousands of paragraphs, hundreds of scenes, but I never showed you one single sentence. I was afraid to know for sure that you thought my work was my hustle—a shiny, indulgent waste of time. But more than that, I didn't want you to know that I wanted you to be better at being human.

I didn't want you to see that I saw in the real you someone I never wanted to be, a shiftless paroled "nigger" worthy of only hollow awe or rabid disgust, a smiling "nigger" who fought a few good rounds before getting his ass whupped by white supremacy and quaint multiculturalism over and over again. Uncle Jimmy, I knew that you were slowly killing yourself. And predictably, I knew that I would become you.

I hated you and me both for that.

This is a shameful admission, a confession that is even more sour with indulgent guilt when I acknowledge that all of the women in my writing who are partially based on the characters of Grandmama, Mama, Aunt Sue, and Aunt Linda are far less moving, round, and paradoxical than the actual women themselves. And this has less to do with my writing than it does with my love and understanding of these human beings, and our love and understanding of each other. I loved the women in our family enough to ask them questions. They loved me enough

153

to answer those questions, often with questions of their own. I wrote to them. They wrote back.

Echo.

Honestly, I don't know if I ever asked you any real questions other than why you looked so happy in your Vietnam pictures when I was ten, and why you said, "There's some fine b—es on Earth," when you picked me up from grad school when I was twenty-four.

My creating interesting American characters based on you to fit the specifications of a paragraph doesn't make me despicable; it makes me an American writer. What makes me despicable is that one of the responsibilities of American writers is to broaden the confines, sensibilities, and generative capacity of American literature by broadening the audience to whom we write, and hoping that broadened audience writes back with brutal imagination, magic, and brilliance.

Echo.

You can't really explore the terror and wonder of being born, as Baldwin says, "captive in the supposed Promised Land" if you never conceive of the captives as the crucial critics, not simply consumers or objects, of your work. I started writing this book to you before you died. I was in desperate need of echo, and I'd convinced myself that the only way to live was to write through what was helping me kill myself. I don't only wish you could have read this book, Uncle Jimmy; I wish you could have written back to us.

Anyway, only a fool doesn't actively regret. I wish we could have waded in the awkward acceptance that we are neither African nor conventionally American; neither subhuman nor superhuman; neither tragic nor comic; neither defeated nor victorious. I wish we could have affirmed our awareness that our Blackness and our Southerness are both perpetual burden and benefit, our masculinity and femininity something that must be reckoned with, but never reconciled.

Mostly, Uncle Jimmy, I wish you could have told me that we are fucked up, and much of the nation has always wanted it that way, but we owe it to our teachers and our children to imagine new routes into beauty, health, compassion, citizenry, and American imagination. We owe it to each other to love and insist on meaningful revision until the day we die.

That's what I needed to tell you when you were alive. That's what I needed you to show me. That's what I need help believing.

One night, while revising *Long Division*, I thanked God that you weren't my father, while feeling like the luckiest nephew in the world because I could call someone as tortured as you my uncle. I wondered who and what I really would have become without you as my warning. I wondered how your life would have been different if I had told you I loved you. What would you have done differently with your life if you had really believed me? What would we have both felt? If you wrote truthfully to me, how would you start and end your letter? What senses would you write through? What would you discover?

Uncle Jimmy, no matter how I contort these words and squeeze the mess out of my memory and imagination, we will never ever know. This book is a love letter written a few years too late. I am sorry I didn't love you.

Your nephew,
Kiese

Dear Jimmy,

Although you have transitioned to the other side of life, we still feel your presence and pray for you. Your sister Linda, misses how you'd greet her with "Hello sis, how Vegas treating you?" She misses listening to you sing the blues. Your sister Mary misses your face, your gait, your love of summer sandals. She misses your hugs and your bad taste in Christmas presents. She hates that Mama will never see you again and she is sure your death took some of Mama's resilience with you. I am not sure about that. Mama is weaker since you've passed. I know that's true. But we all are weaker since you've gone. Our nephew, Kiese, thinks he lives with your ghost. I try to tell him that he's always lived with your spirit.

I have learned more about you in death than I knew in life. Little did I know that a young lady you used to smoke crack with has come to know Jesus and become a part of my ministry. We never know what our lives will bring to those we leave behind.

I never questioned your love for me or for the family. I knew you loved us, but I was never sure if you loved yourself. Life has a way of rewinding itself.

You once said to me from your hospital bed that it wasn't so much the crack as the sex that kept you getting high. I left the hospital after midnight out of frustration and disappointment at how you did not value your life. I said to you, "If you don't care about you, why should I?" I walked out of the hospital wondering what I could do to help my brother. God gave me the answer. "Love him," He said. "Demand greatness of him and give him to me." I learned another lesson from you that night. Love requires forgiveness, truth, high expectations, and patience.

You taught me something very important that night. You taught me that love without acceptance and understanding isn't love. I told you the next morning that I would not give you money under any circumstance. If you were hungry, I would feed you. If you were lonely, I would share scriptures and words of encouragement. But I would not give you my hard-earned cash to purchase drugs.

You fought your demons, Jimmy. Your nephew and I are still fighting ours. This young lady who knew you called me crying a little past midnight. She wanted me to know about you. She told me that while you were getting high you encouraged her to reclaim her life and her children. She said, "Mr. Jimmy was a good man. He tried to help people. Often people took his kindness as a weakness." She told me of how you gave her money to buy her children clothes and how you counseled her about the importance of raising her children and setting a good example for them.

I want you to know she took your advice. She is now off crack and her children are living with her. Life is a struggle at times but she is determined to make it. You made a difference in her life. You made a difference in mine.

I was so glad that the last time that we spoke, you told me you didn't hate white people anymore. For the first time in my life, you seemed to be at peace. Peace with yourself, Mama, the family, and peace with your God.

You didn't look like the man who had grown old too soon, with the stressors of life written in every wrinkle in your face. You did not look like a man with less than 90 percent lung and heart capacity. Somehow, some way, your youth had returned. Your dignity was restored and you had become the man you wanted to be all your life. You looked like the handsome brother of your youth. Mary commented as we waved goodbye on that Fourth of July, "Do you think Jimmy is about to die?" I did not respond, but I knew that life as you knew it had come to its final hours.

One day when I was leaving the VA Hospital, you told me you wanted me to preach at your funeral. I told you that you were crazy and that was one thing that I would never do. Well, you never ever know what love and God makes possible.

On July 12, I stood looking into a casket that belonged to my brother. I stepped from the clothes of being your sister and put on the robes of an ambassador for God. I shared the hope of a man who struggled, won, and lost, who was often too lonely to face life while married to a pipe filled with crack. While cleaning out your home, I found your journal. I read your words and I felt your pain in ways that I will never be able to express. What you could not articulate in life you spoke to us from your journals. Your writing meant so much to your nephew. You wrote, "I have stolen from my mother, hurt my sisters and I want to stop but I don't know how." On another page you wrote, "I don't know the person I have become. God help me."

Your heart was good but you forgot to guard it. You killed yourself slowly because of this. The heart is the true measure of a man or woman. I loved you and I know that you knew I loved you. We all have addictions. Some are just more obvious to the eye. We are all dying, but we are all living. The key is to live with as much dignity as you can and never ever bring other people down because you've given up on life. Your work is finished but your worth is still being revealed. Your life was not in vain, Jimmy. You made a difference. You helped our mother find the strength and the courage to fight another day and your words inspired her to change her life. I think that is the true measure of our worth and why God put us on the earth. Have we made life better for others by lending a hand, a heart, a word, a song, hope for despair—and always, always shared the gift of love? We may be broken, but God knows how to mend broken hearts and spirits. I have been made better by knowing you, brother, and I thank you for the lessons along the way. Mama misses you. We know you had to leave us. We hate that you had to leave her.

Love always,
Your sister Sue

A Note on the Author

Born and raised in Jackson, Mississippi, Kiese Laymon is the author of the novel *Long Division* and the memoir *Heavy*.